Cooking
Aboard
Your
RV

Janet Groene

Ragged Mountain Press
Camden, Maine

Published by Ragged Mountain Press

10   9   8   7   6   5   4   3   2

Library of Congress Cataloging-in-Publication Data
Groene, Janet.
      Cooking aboard your RV / Janet Groene
          p.   cm.
      Includes index.
      ISBN 0-87742-339-3
      1. Cookery. 2. Recreational vehicles.
          3. Camping.
I. Title.
TX840.m6G76 1993
641.5--dc20   92-30798
                                        CIP

Questions regarding the content of this book should
be addressed to:
Ragged Mountain Press
P.O. Box 220
Camden, ME 04843

For every book sold, Ragged Mountain Press will
make a contribution to an environmental cause.

Cooking Aboard Your RV is printed on 60-pound
Renew Opaque Vellum, which contains 50 percent
recycled waste paper (preconsumer) and 10 percent
postconsumer waste paper.

Printed by Fairfield Graphics, Fairfield, PA.
Design by Patrice M. Rossi.
Production by Molly Mulhern.
Edited by Jim Babb, Dorathy Chocensky, and Pamela
Benner.

Some of these recipes appeared previously in *Family
Motor Coaching* magazine and are reprinted here
with permission.

CONTENTS
••••

To Mom, who proofread and prodded, tested and suggested, spelled and smelled, tasted and taught. And to Gordon, who, by being there, makes my every meal a banquet.

Introduction

Longtime readers of my food articles know that my first cookbook, *Cooking on the Go*, was written for sailors and campers who have no ovens or refrigeration. Increasingly, however, I've sensed a demand for an additional cookbook written for the unique needs of the RV cook. In our RVs we have many luxuries that were unheard of in campgrounds a generation ago. We have ovens, refrigerators with freezer compartments, hot and cold running water, double sinks, and probably microwave ovens. All may be in miniature, but we have almost all the comforts of home.

Most of us also have a few basic small appliances such as blenders, food processors, toasters, coffee makers, and electric skillets. We have 110-volt power at least part of the time, and we're able to do things with propane and 12-volt power that kitchen cooks can't.

What we usually do *not* have are dishwashers, garbage disposals, unlimited water, full-size stoves and ovens with broilers, enough cupboard or counter space, or any of the specialty appliances and cookware found in today's kitchens.

In this book, I'll celebrate the many conveniences that modern RVs offer but, as an active RV traveler, I will also remember the problems and limitations of RV cooking.

Among my personal peeves are recipes for "one-dish" meals that require many pans and bowls before they end up in one pot, "quick" recipes that start with a step that takes hours ("boil and pick meat from one bushel blue crabs"), fancy recipes that call for exotic ingredients that I'm unlikely to carry aboard, and dishes that require great quantities of water for cooking or rinsing.

If you're like me, you want recipes for foods that are good to eat and to look at, healthful and nutritious, and fairly quick and easy to cook without making undue mess, and recipes that mesh with the casual, active, chic, and health-conscious outdoor lifestyle.

In presenting my recipes and instructions, I'm assuming that you already know the basics of cooking. I didn't want to take up space with lengthy explanations of how to test for doneness, how to hard boil eggs, or how to cut shortening into dry ingredients. If cooking terms are new to you, get any good, basic cookbook, such as *Joy of Cooking, Betty Crocker's Cookbook,* or the *Good Housekeeping Illustrated Cookbook.*

Writing a book for the RV cook is a tall order because we are all different. I know many RV families who love to gather around the campfire and cook as they did in their tenting days. Some want quick recipes that are ready to serve in minutes. Others prefer slow, fragrant soups and stews that cook all day in a crockpot or oven while the family fishes or hikes.

Some RV cooks are classic cordon bleu chefs, maintaining the highest cuisine standards. (One of my friends carries a set of crystal wine glasses aboard, which cost about $60 per stem.) Others couldn't care less about food. They'd rather live on apples and peanut butter, and spend their time reading or playing.

Some RV campers are vegetarians, diabetics, or weight watchers. Some are brawny outdoorsmen who need more calories in a day than others consume in a week. Some have finicky or allergic kids. Some live off the land. Some live on canned ravioli and TV dinners. Some insist on carrying a clay cooking pot or automatic steam cooker or electric potato peeler—items that most of us never use, even at home.

Despite our differences, all of us eat. And to most of us the preparing and sharing of mealtimes is one of the most rewarding and unifying of campground pleasures. In remembering our sameness, and respecting our differences, I hoped to assemble a collection of recipes that will work for most RV travelers most of the time.

—Janet Groene
(say GRAYnee)

CHAPTER ONE

How Green Was My Galley

In the pecking order that environmental purists create for themselves, RV camping usually comes in very close to the bottom because we are perceived as luxury-loving sissies who bring all our conveniences to the wilderness with us.

Let's look at some of our good points. For one thing, we often do more "from scratch" cooking than other campers (meaning we're using less packaging) because we have more facilities with us. While we're traveling in our RVs, we are living in miniature. Meanwhile, the air conditioner, furnace, water heater, self-cleaning oven, automatic dishwasher, garbage disposal, and other appliances at home are turned off.

It's our outdoors too, so we are as careful as any other campers about recycling, waste disposal, and water conservation.

In many cases, we are using fewer campground resources. We are providing much of our own energy in the form of generator power, 12-volt battery power (some of which is often provided by roof-mounted solar panels), and propane. We may bring in some or all of our own water and take out some or all of our own wastewater.

Many "primitive" campers plug into campground power to run their electric blankets, hot plates, heaters, corn poppers, and lights. We RVers, by contrast, know the price of energy because we have to charge our own batteries, refill our own propane tanks, and fuel and maintain our own generators.

Because most of us have brought all our own facilities with us, we don't ask the park to provide us with hot showers, firewood, grills, and flush toilets. If we do play a television or stereo, we can close the doors and windows so others don't have to listen to our choice of program, unlike those who sleep under the stars and inflict their boom boxes and smoky fires on everyone.

It's true that some RV campers are slobs, just as some tenters and some backpackers are slobs. But RV campers have made a big investment in their units, far more than has to be made in any other form of camping, which makes us deeply concerned about the preservation of our camping resources. We're in for the long haul and have put our money where our mouth is.

We *can* take it with us. That means we can also pack much of it *out* with us rather than burning, burying, or leaving our trash for the rangers to haul away.

Here are some random ideas for RV cookery, conservation style.

- A pressure cooker is a great energy saver, and in many cases is quicker than a microwave. It uses less fuel and, because cooking times are shorter, puts less burden on the air conditioning.

- Carry powdered and concentrated drink mixes and reconstitute them in reusable containers. Don't carry bottled juices and canned sodas. You're paying to transport heavy, disposable containers filled with what is essentially water.

- Install a good water treatment system in the RV, and you'll have safe drinking water anywhere you go without having to lug along bottled water.

- Long-life milk in cardboard cartons leaves less waste than a plastic bottle. Powdered milk is the most compact of all, leaving the least trash. The secret to making it palatable is to mix it two to three hours before drinking it. Because protein is reluctant to combine with water, a "steeping" time is needed to eliminate the chalky texture of reconstituted milk.

- If you must use foods that come in bulky packaging, repackage them at home in reusable containers—crackers and cookies into tin boxes, cereals and grains into glass or plastic jars. Such containers also help preserve freshness.

•Use nature's packaging: whole, fresh fruits and vegetables, garlic by the braid, nuts in the shell, sausages and cheeses in natural casings, real eggs in real shells, and whole grains.

•When you buy produce in plastic net bags, save the bags to use as scrubbers. They are as effective as steel wool but won't scratch delicate surfaces. Plastic net is also good for scrubbing bugs off the nose of the RV.

•Don't use steel wool or other cleansers that could leave a gritty residue. When you're skimping on water, a lengthy rinse isn't always possible.

•In drought areas where your gray water might save a tree, use it as allowed to water worthy plants. Water used to cook pasta, rinse sprouts, wash greens, or boil eggs can be drained from the pot into the dishpan and used as part of the wash-up water.

•Buy only environmentally responsible RV chemicals. Baking soda is an effective, food-quality galley cleanser. Vinegar or ammonia and water makes glass sparkle. A cut lemon dipped in salt cleans copper. Soft soap rubbed on the outside of a cooking pot before it's put over the fire will wash off, taking campfire carbon with it.

•Minimize the use of chemical sprays by making maximum use of fly paper and screens.

•Don't use toilet chemicals that contain formaldehyde, or non-potable antifreezes in drinking water tanks.

•Instead of buying small sizes for galley use, save small containers at home to make up weekend-size portions of galley staples.

•Where possible, buy or repackage spreadables such as peanut butter, margarine, mustard, ketchup, mayonnaise, and jelly in squeeze containers. It's more sanitary to squeeze them onto the bread, and you don't have extra spreaders and spoons to wash.

•Old-fashioned, basic ingredients are almost always the most nutritious and compact, with the least packaging. Bring plain popcorn, not fancy packaged types. Snack on freshly popped corn instead of greasy, bulky potato chips. European-style crisp-breads are preferable to snack crackers. They come in simple paper wrappers instead of bulky boxes with plastic liners, and they contain little or no fat. You can carry a serving of raw oatmeal or other cooked cereal in a fraction of the space taken by ready-to-eat cereals. A simple bag of raw rice will feed an army; a big box of instant rice feeds one family one meal.

•Invest in plastic egg carriers. Buy eggs in bulk, not in puffy plastic containers, and carry them safely in these reusable cases.

•Buy cookware with the best and most durable nonstick coatings (my favorite is the new T-Fal Resistal). In many cases, no dish-washing is required. They wipe clean with a paper towel.

•Start a collection at home of freshly laundered rags, preferably linen or cotton. I call mine the One Mo' Time Collection. When folding and sorting laundry, I take out any towel, sheet, or other natural-fiber item that is good for only one more use (as a rag), and put it into a clean sack consigned to the camper. Instead of reaching for a paper towel, I reach for a clean rag. When it's soiled, it becomes biodegradable trash.

•Disposables are a way of life in camping but they add cost, bulk, and trash problems to the trip. Eliminate paper cups by buying a mug for each member of the family and labeling it with a name, favorite team, or some other marking. Make everyone responsible for rinsing out his own mug after each use and returning it to the cupboard.

•Use insulated containers to keep things cold or hot. Fill an ice bucket with ice cubes for cocktail hour so the refrigerator door doesn't have to be opened repeatedly. Fill a thermos with coffee or hot water. Use natural coolers (e.g. the six-pack in the stream) and heaters. (The dashboard becomes a greenhouse when the sun is shin-ing in. Set the yogurt, defrost the roast, or proof the dough there.)

•The most effective bleach for natural fibers, especially linen, is sunshine. Dry dishcloths and dishtowels in the sun.

•Read labels. Most of us use far more of every detergent, cleaner, and chemical than is necessary for the task at hand.

•Make an awning or sunshade for the area where the refrigerator coils are, so the unit won't have to work unnecessarily hard.

•It probably isn't necessary to leave the hotwater heater on all the time in camp. (It's never run on the highway, where the open flame is a hazard.) Most RVs have a small, quick-recovery unit that can be turned on only as needed for showers and dishwashing.

•Invest in a solar battery-charger. It's a silent servant, working unseen on the RV roof. The more panels you can afford, the longer you can linger in the wilderness without starting the engine or generator.

•Minimize your dependence on an AC generator as much as possible. Generators cost money to buy, fuel, and maintain, and they generate fumes and noise as well as electricity. Many galley appliances, including a Waring blender called the Tailgater, can be found in 12-volt versions; others, such as Nordic Ware's waffle maker, are available in stovetop models that operate atop the gas stove; still others can be run off your 12-volt "house" battery system through an inverter. Even a microwave oven can be run off an inverter *if* you have a large enough inverter and a big enough battery bank to supply it.

•Learn about fireless cookers. Various commercial types, such as Roc Crock, are available through camping supply stores, or you can make your own by using an ice chest filled with newspapers, pillows, or straw pallets, leaving just a small space for a pot. Insulation must be many inches thick, and must surround the pot tightly. Some models have insulation alone; others incorporate a hot stone that is heated atop the stove before it's placed in the cooker with the cooking pot. Bring a heavy pot of stew or soaked beans to a boil, place it in a fireless cooker, and six to eight hours later it's cooked to perfection.

•Experiment with manifold cooking, in which foil-wrapped foods cook in surplus engine heat underway. It all depends on what room you have available under the hood, and what temperatures are maintained there, so some experimenting will be needed before you perfect the pot roast recipe that will work on *your* engine, in the space available in *your* engine compartment.

•Surplus engine heat can also be channeled to the hotwater heater in some RVs. The system is used more commonly on boats, so you might ask a marine center about the feasibility of using a similar heat exchanger in your RV.

•Grow your own sprouts and you'll have fresh, natural greens everywhere you go. Because a tablespoon or two of seeds swells to a quart of sprouts, you can carry an entire produce patch in a few ounces of weight.

•Everything you carry in your RV costs petrodollars to accelerate, cruise, and brake. Buy everything possible in a powdered, dehydrated, concentrated, dried, boneless, or compressed form. If it comes in both glass and plastic (liquor, wine, mustard, vinegar, sodas, mayo), plastic is lighter and less breakable.

•Think in terms of portions per pound and per cubic inch. You can feed four to six with a tiny jar of dried chipped beef or a 12-ounce can of corned beef.

•Although individual packaging costs more and makes for more trash, it also makes a contribution to your RV camp-out. Individual packets save work, time, and waste. They control portions for you (how many bowls of cereal can you get from a 17-ounce box?), and they keep every morsel fresh until the package is opened. In some cases, it's a fair tradeoff.

•Pay heed to fire laws in each campground. They vary according to area and season. Where fires are allowed, stick to wood, cardboard, and paper. Don't burn plastics, foils, or garbage. An electric charcoal-fire starter is safer than petroleum-based starters, and pollutes the air less.

•Recycling practices are different in every community. Do your best to separate recyclables in the way that is best for *this* campground or community. It may be quite different from the way you sort things at home.

•If you have a choice when purchasing a new RV, or can convert your present one, get a stove hood that has an overboard exhaust rather than a recirculating filter. Filters are only moderately effective on odors and spatters, and they don't remove moisture or heat at all, so your air conditioner works harder.

•Where you have filters that are to be washed or changed, be scrupulous about it. Don't forget the air conditioners (both automotive and rooftop), stove exhaust, furnace, and vacuum cleaner. Clogged filters cost energy.

•Don't use drain cleaners. They could damage the RV's plumbing or tanks, and they add chemicals to the environment. Fit all drains with good basket strainers. When stoppages occur, clear them with a plumber's helper.

•Use rechargeable batteries and rechargeable appliances.

•Buy refills for pump- and spray-type soaps and cleaners.

About Living Off the Land

Trying native foods is one of the most exciting and interesting ways for serious travelers to enjoy different areas to the fullest. Such foods aren't always lip-smacking tasty and often are not easy to find or prepare. But like them or not, some experimenting is educational and fun.

Once, walking in the Indiana woods in autumn, a friend of ours picked just one perfectly ripe pawpaw and introduced us to the "Indiana banana." It was delectable. My father and I once spent hours finding and preparing cattails in a way recommended by a popular book. They were simply awful.

Yet elderberries, shunned in some parts of the country, where they are thought to be poisonous, were among our favorite finds. So are wild persimmons. In some areas, wild edibles are so abundant that you can harvest a "mess" without guilt. Dig clams, tong for oysters, cast nets for shrimp.

Gleaning is another way to live off the land, when farmers invite people into their fields after the harvest to take whatever leavings they can find. By the end of a season's camping in North Carolina, we had cupboards filled with canned and dried apples from orchards that commercial growers had abandoned.

U-pick farms are found throughout the nation. Watch for road signs, read ads in shopper tabloids, or write each state's Department of Agriculture to see if they publish a list of such farms. Prices are not always dirt cheap, but you're able to pick the very best of the crop at its peak freshness.

In our camper we've always carried a few books about living off the land. However, as populations balloon and pressure on our wilderness increases, responsible campers are more careful about harvesting nature's bounty. In some parks it's illegal to pick anything. It's forbidden nationwide to pick sea oats, a cereal once savored.

In any area it's irresponsible to take more than a modest share. In some places, permits are required to harvest wild edibles such as stone crabs or wild rice.

Never forget that most land belongs to someone. Poaching game, pinching watermelons from farm fields, or picking from roadside orchards and groves is *stealing*. In areas where farm families have to live all year on the proceeds of one harvest, officials are not amused by tourists who help themselves. At worst, you can pay fines totalling hundreds of thousands of dollars. At best, you could get a butt full of rock salt.

In some cases, it's too dangerous to live off the land—or sea—with its pollutants, residues, "red tides," and mercury. And even experts are sometimes fooled by wild mushrooms. Proceed with full knowledge of the area, its flora and fauna, its folkways, and its current laws.

Some foods, such as pokeweed, dandelion, or cactus are so common in some areas, almost any child can identify them. Others are uncommon even in areas where they grow, so it takes a little more investigating to make sure they're safe to eat.

The best thing about regional harvests is that they give us travelers a new tool to make friends. Strike up conversations with locals, especially senior citizens. Listen to the lore of regional foods. Some, as in the case of our "poison" elderberries, is utter nonsense; some is made up on the spot, I'm sure, to impress a damfool outsider who won't know the difference anyway. The rest is pure gold, 24-carat Americana in its sweetest form.

Listen and learn, and your family's love for the land will grow and grow.

CHAPTER TWO

Furnishing the Kitchen on Wheels

How can you feed shark-size appetites out of a minnow-size RV galley? It all begins with the choice of equipment that is exactly right for the task. Not garage-sale junk. Not the stuff that isn't good enough to use in the kitchen anymore. And not cheap dimestore pans with battered, ill-fitting lids.

It's tempting to furnish the RV with castoffs. This is hardly raw-boned camping in the rough, but it is different, and difficult, and RV cookery is tough enough without additional roadblocks. No matter how luxurious your galley, it's still a galley with too little storage space, limited water, fewer conveniences than at home, and never enough countertop area. You need the right equipment in the right sizes, amounts, and materials. Nothing more, nothing less.

A basic inventory might include:

Balloon whisk. For quick mixing jobs without an electric beater, it will do a more thorough job than a spoon and is easier to wash than an egg beater. I carry a large one for batters and a tiny one for small tasks such as whisking herbs into mayo or sour cream.

Bucket. You need a scrub bucket anyway, so invest in a high-quality stainless steel pail that can also be used as a lobster or pasta pot, laundry basin, and carryall.

9

Can opener. Spend the extra money to get a double-geared type; both wheels turn together, transporting the can as the cut is made.

Cutting board. Get one that doubles as a sink fill-in piece to increase your counter space.

Dishes. The lighter and more breakproof, the better. Avoid heavy pottery and ironstone, which cost fuel dollars to transport, and disposables, which are expensive both to your budget and to the environment. Favor melamines or Corelle.

Ice bucket. If you get an ice bucket that can withstand hot temperatures as well as cold, you can use it for both. Keep ice cubes on hand to cut down on traffic in and out of the refrigerator. When you're cooking a meal of many courses and are short of burners, cook one dish ahead of time and keep it hot in an ice bucket.

I once met a camper who brought her potatoes to a hard boil, simmered them until crisp-tender, and then transferred them to an insulated container/ice bucket. The potatoes continued to cook, and her burners were free. If you try this, use only an ice bucket that has a heat-tolerant liner.

Ice chests. Keep separate ice chests for fish and bait and, if your family drinks a lot of canned beer or soda, another one for that. Keep the mess, smells, and traffic out of your refrigerator. When you don't need it as an ice chest, use it as a catchall. Big, box-style ice chests also serve as outdoor seats, tables, and work surfaces.

Use ice chests for hot foods, too, to carry hot take-out meals to the campground. One Kansas family stops for Chinese food on Friday nights on the way out of town in the RV. The cartons, piping hot, are put in an ice chest lined thickly with newspapers and preheated by placing a hot pan inside. The food is still hot and ready to eat when they reach the campsite.

Use a warm ice chest for raising dough and culturing yogurt by putting either in the chest with a bottle of very hot water. Close tightly and let the heat from the water maintain the right warmth.

Knives. Get a good, basic set of knives with a holder that will keep them safe on the road. Rattling around in a drawer will dull and nick the edges.

Measurers. Plastic measuring cups do nothing but measure. Instead, get stainless steel measuring cups, which can also be used for melting butter or heating syrup over a burner set on low. Large Pyrex measuring cups can also be used as mixing bowls, pitchers, microwave cookware, and bakeware.

Milk crate(s). Now readily available in heavy-duty plastic, these carryalls come in rigid or folding models. They can be used in many ways. Round up all your cookout equipment in one, canned goods in another. Use them as "drawers" on an unused bunk and fill them with linens or clothing. Use them as dividers in big, cavernous holds under dinette seats and in the RV's "basement."

Use an upturned empty crate as an entry step to your RV. Dirt on your shoes will drop through the holes and onto the ground.

If you're doing dishes outdoors, give them a good sudsing, place them in a plastic crate, and hose to rinse. Then air dry in the breeze.

Mixing bowl(s). A nest of high-quality stainless steel mixing bowls is a lifetime investment. Get at least one super-size bowl for popcorn, big salads, and big mixing jobs. When not in use, it can be used as a fruit bowl or catchall.

Mugs. Instead of spending money on disposables, get a distinctive mug for each member of the family. Each person can use and rinse his or her own mug. It will need a sudsy hot wash only once a day or so.

Pitcher. Rather than carry heavy, bulky drinks in bottles and cans, rely on juice concentrates and dry mixes such as Kool Aid, Crystal Light, and iced tea. If you have a pitcher, you can mix them as needed.

Pots and pans. Consider weight, versatility, cleanability, and stackability. Iron is heavy and it rusts, but there is nothing like it for campfire cooking. (I don't recommend it for stovetop cooking because of its poor heat-transfer qualities.) Cast aluminum is best for slow, even heat in stovetop baking; stamped aluminum provides instant heat transfer for sautéing.

Some microware can be used in conventional ovens too, so some RV cooks carry no other bakeware. Stackable, steamer-type pots can cook three or more foods at once. I like a Hackman steamer for the stovetop and Tupperware's Stackables for the microwave.

A pressure cooker saves time and fuel. Nonstick linings make cleanup a breeze; my favorite is a new T-Fal coating called Resistal. Consider getting a wok—stir-fry cooking is quick and practical. For short trips all the foods can be cut up and packaged at home.

What is best? My advice is to start with one or two thick, lidded pots and a high-quality, lidded, nonstick skillet. Then add pans as needed. I emphasize that the pans (except for sauté pans) should be heavy, in seeming contradiction to the appeal of lightweight galleyware, because the RV chef may have to do a lot of burner shuffling to make a five-course meal on a two- or three-burner stove. Heavy pots hold heat better, even in cold or windy weather.

Rechargeable appliances. Consider getting a cordless electric beater so you'll have full-time electric mixing even when you're not on generator or shore power. Cordless can openers and electric knives also are available. Such appliances need regular recharging; they're not for the cook who goes long periods without AC. Ours is mounted permanently, so it's always on charge when we're plugged in. Although rechargeables have come many miles since their early days, when they were quirky and underpowered, they still rely on regular recharging. Never put one away discharged and don't leave them in the RV during long layups.

Shakers. These can be nothing more than wide-mouth canning, peanut butter, or peanut jars. Avoid lids with cardboard inserts; those with rubbery inner seals are the most leakproof. I keep one or two large shakers for mixing pancake batter or instant pudding. Smaller shakers are good for whipping eggs for omelets or making salad dressings. Simply dump all ingredients into the jar, lid tightly, shake to mix, and pour. Instead of having to wash a bowl, spatula, and beater, just put a little water in the jar with some detergent and a few pebbles or a teaspoon of raw rice, and shake until it's scrubbed clean. Rinse and dry. If you're on short water rations and have a few jars saved, throw them into the recycling bin instead of washing them.

Silverware. Two-piece tableware with plastic or wood handles is inexpensive and good looking, but germs and goo can hide in the seams. Get high-quality, seamless silverware with a smooth finish. It will come clean more easily, with less water, in hand dishwashing.

Small appliances. Try to find electric appliances that do more than one thing. Tefal makes a unique toaster-broiler. Toaster ovens come in many sizes and styles. Oster offers a mixer that has attachments including food processor, salad maker, juicer, and blender. West Bend's slow cooker comprises a four-quart pot, a base that can be used as an electric griddle, and a heatproof glass lid that is just the right size for baking cornbread or a one-layer cake.

Thermos bottles. You can save time, trouble, and energy if you keep a container of hot water and one of ice water or iced tea on hand. When cold drinks are handy in their own containers, your family members aren't into the refrigerator every two minutes. With hot water you can make coffee, tea, bouillon, gelatin, instant cocoa, and many other treats without lighting the stove or heating a kettle of water.

The Little (and Not So Little) Luxuries

The marketplace overflows with tempting kitchen accessories and countertop appliances. As a food writer as well as a galley cook, I try most of them with the galley in mind. While every new appliance is useful to some cooks some of the time, RV cooks have to make tough choices about what to take and what to leave at home. Every holiday season seems to bring a new crop of small appliances. Many of them wind up under the tree this year, and at the garage sale next year.

Remember the donut-maker craze a few years ago? And the powered cookie press? Some appliances enjoy a brief sensation, disappear, and resurface every few years. Juicers have made a big comeback recently. Other favorites, such as the crock cooker, never fade away. Still others, such as the new automatic bread makers, pasta makers, and espresso machines, are a passing fad in some households but become necessities in others. Here are some considerations in choosing small appliances for the RV galley. In the end, however, the only considerations are your own cooking style, the priorities you put on your limited storage space, and the feasibility of using those appliances within the limits of space, weight, and electrical power available to you.

If you already have any of these small appliances, you might try them aboard the RV one at a time. It makes every trip's menus more interesting if you focus on homemade breads this time, deep-fry treats the next, and daily homemade sorbets after that.

I've rated these appliances electrically Low, Medium, and High. Those requiring Low or Medium power can be run, at least for short periods, on small or medium inverters; those rated High need large inverters, shore power, or generator power. Keep in mind the one drawback shared by all countertop appliances: Unless it's bolted down, it can't stay on the counter underway. It must be stowed securely each time you drive away.

Models designed for under-counter installation in the kitchen are often chosen for RV use. Small appliances that come in under-counter mounts include toaster ovens, coffee makers, small microwaves, and radio/television sets. Another appliance that can be mounted permanently, and is standard equipment on some high-end RVs, is a multipurpose tool that operates off a motor that is installed under the counter (Nutone is one brand). Only the small drive, to which you can attach a blender, food processor, and other accessories, is visible on the counter.

Here are some appliance pros and cons.

Automatic Bread Maker

What it is: A completely automated bread "factory" in which you place all the ingredients. About two hours later, a perfect loaf of bread is turned out.

Pro: Because a daily supply of fresh bread is one of camping's biggest shopping problems, this allows an unending supply of fresh and fragrant "staff of life." Because high-quality bakery bread is difficult to find, especially in campground stores, this provides a healthy alternative to white fluff.

Con: Heavy for its size. Requires Medium-High AC. Computer operated, so any AC interruption stops the cycle and requires manual completion of the loaf. Makes only one, two- or three-cup loaf at a time; not practical for larger families.

Blender

What it is: A tiny, very-high-speed blade pulverizes food and ice.

Pro: Small in size, available in powerful 12-volt model (Waring's Tailgater), modest AC needs allows 110-volt models to be used on most inverters. Invaluable for making frozen drinks, health drinks, purees, baby food. Easy to clean.

Con: Cannot whip cream or egg whites. Limited uses. Some cooks find the food processor does most things they used to do with a blender, and more.

Coffee Maker

What it is: The automatic coffee maker rates second only to the toaster as the most essential item in many kitchens.

Pro: Convenient. Standard equipment on some RV models. Available for under-counter installation (although the coffee pot itself will probably have to be stowed underway).

Con: Medium-High AC needs. Programmable models not practical unless you have full-time AC. Not multipurpose; only makes coffee. Ground coffee less compact to carry than instant.

Crock Cooker

What it is: Many types and sizes are available, all of them using very low heat so that long, slow cooking is assured without stirring or supervision.

Pro: Because models come in so many sizes, you can get the capacity that's right for your family. Some models, such as the West Bend, sit atop a burner that serves as a separate griddle. Ideal for soups, tough meats, dried beans, culturing yogurt.

Con: Requires Low-Medium AC. Some units don't get hot enough to pre-brown meat. Moderately heavy.

Deep Fryer

What it is: The new types cook with less mess and less fat to make homemade donuts, French fries, fritters, and much more.

Pro: If your family demands a lot of fried foods, you'll be able to cook with more healthful ingredients if you make your own. Quick, convenient. Some models combine frying with pressure to make fast-food-style chicken and fish. Fresh donuts or French fries are a great attention-getter in campgrounds.

Con: Comparatively heavy, messy, Medium-High AC needs. Limited uses. Cooking oil is expensive; filtering and saving it for re-use is cumbersome.

Electric Skillet

What it is: A thermostat-controlled electric frying pan.

Pro: Available in many sizes, from miniatures large enough to fry a couple of eggs to large fryer-roasters with domed lids. Can be used to bake, fry, roast. Available in both 110- and 12-volt models.

Con: To me, the electric skillet is overrated for RV cooking because it can only bake, braise, or fry. If, on the other hand, you carry an electric buffet burner (hot plate), you have a thermostat-controlled cooker that can be used under a coffee maker, corn popper, tea kettle, skillet, saucepan, griddle, double boiler, Dutch oven, stovetop toaster, wok, or pressure cooker. In short, the electric skillet is an extra burner with limited abilities, so why not add an extra electric burner in the form of a hot plate?

Food Processor

What it is: Full-feature models have a knife blade to mince and grind, a paddle for mixing, and two or more cutting wheels that shred and grate. Small and battery models have very limited uses, such as chopping parsley.

Pro: A necessity to many modern cooks. Modest AC needs, many uses.

Con: Not easy to clean. Comparatively heavy. Smaller than a full-size electric mixer with attachments but can't do as much.

Ice Cream Maker

What it is: Makes homemade ice cream, sherbert.

Pro: Ice cream is everyone's favorite dessert, but it's not easy to keep on hand in the limited space of an RV freezer. Allows you to favor more healthful ingredients and eliminate chemical additives. Many types available, from hand-crank models to fully automatic appliances. Make sure you understand what you have to supply. Most campgrounds carry ice by the bag; some ice cream makers must be placed inside the freezer, where you simply may not have room. Electric models require Low AC. A great team sport in camp.

Con: Bulky, hard to clean. Ingredients are bulky too, although some are available in powdered form. Where salt is used, resulting runoff is very corrosive and is not good for surrounding trees and plants.

Juicer

What it is: Another of the appliances that reaches fad status periodically, it reduces whole fresh fruits and vegetables to juice.

Pro: Very popular with people who are sold on "juicing" as a healthful diet. Extracts more nutrients from foods than do juicer attachments.

Con: Medium AC requirement. Comparatively heavy. Limited uses unless you're on a juice diet. Hard to clean. Some foods require peeling first.

Kitchen Wand

What it is: Its high-speed blender-type blade can be used to whip and chop in any container you choose. Popular in Europe.

Pro: Very light, compact, versatile. Low AC draw. Easy to clean; can be used in a disposable jar or paper cup. Introduced through demonstrations and sold at very high prices, but now very affordable in department-store housewares sections.

Con: Requires practice to wield one like the professional demonstrators do.

Sandwich Maker

What it is: Modern versions of the old campfire pie iron, these new electric appliances have a nonstick lining that allows messless cooking of filled sandwiches and pastries.

Pro: Small, lightweight, wipes clean with a damp cloth. They make it fun to invent new fillings and wrappers. Can be used for breakfast, lunch, desserts, snacks. Non-electric stovetop models with nonstick finish are available.

Con: Requires Medium-High AC. Limited versatility. Small size makes them impractical for large families.

Smokeless Broiler

What it is: An electric broiler that uses very high heat, and sometimes a reservoir of water, to burn off or capture fat as it drips off meat.

Pro: Because the broilers in most RV ovens are small and ineffective, an alternate method of broiling is always welcome. Can be used indoors or out. Available in many sizes for small or large families. Lightweight. A clean, quick, and convenient alternative to charcoal.

Con: Not easy to clean (although some do have nonstick surfaces). High AC requirement. Bulky. Not versatile; does nothing but broil.

Toaster Oven

What it is: An automatic toaster that also can also be used for baking.

Pro: Many sizes and models are available. Smaller ones are no larger than a pop-up, two-slice toaster, yet can toast bread and bagels, as well as bake potatoes or small meatloaves. Larger ones can be used to roast a whole chicken. Comparatively lightweight. Available with continuous-clean interior, and in under-counter models that can be permanently installed in the RV. Some models broil; a unique Tefal flip-over model is a pop-up toaster in one mode and a broiler in another, but does not bake.

Con: High AC draw.

Turbo Cooker

What it is: A small electric cooker that combines heat with an extremely high-speed air flow.

Pro: Compact, fast as a microwave in most cases, lightweight, can bake and brown bread and many other items that a microwave cannot, moderately easy to clean and stow. Healthful and entirely new way to cook.

Con: Requires AC. Small cooking area (extenders are available for some models). Bakes and broils but cannot cook items with water or small ingredients, which would be sucked into the turbo. It's a unique way to cook, so a new cooking style must be learned.

Beverages: Let's Drink to RV Camping!

Root Beer Float

This is one of my favorite quick desserts because it can be made rich and regal with Ben and Jerry's ice cream, or dietetic using sugar-free root beer and sugar-free, fat-free frozen yogurt. If you have a diabetic in the family, here's one dessert where everyone's looks the same.

Root beer
Vanilla ice cream

Put a scoop of ice cream in a tall glass, and fill the glass with root beer. Add a straw and a spoon, and voilà!

●●●●

Block ice is often available at campgrounds. When you want to make a punch bowl for a hot day, set a block of ice on the end of the picnic table or somewhere where it can drip. Chip a little depression in the top and set a metal pan or bowl in it. Fill the bowl with hot water, and keep refilling until it melts a bowl-shaped depression in the ice. Fill it with your favorite juice or mixed drink. Serve with a ladle.

> Stir ½ t. of your favorite flavor gelatin into each mug of hot tea.
> Or use hot water and 1 t. gelatin mix.

Nog for the 90s

Until scientists can find out why some eggs already contain harmful organisms at the time they are laid, eggnog, Caesar salad, and all the other wonderful recipes that contain raw eggs are verboten. Airline and restaurant cooks and other food-service professionals now use pasteurized eggs; cooking kills the harmful elements.

Here's a safe way to enjoy warming, nourishing eggnog as an afternoon snack, bedtime drink, or dessert on a cold day.

5 c. milk
1 c. liquid egg substitute
½ c. sugar
1 t. vanilla
Dash ground nutmeg
Rum or brandy

Heat the milk over a medium flame, stirring in the sugar and egg substitute until the mixture is hot and somewhat thickened. Remove from heat and stir in the vanilla. Serve warm with rum, kirsch, or brandy if you like. Or chill it, then thin with additional cold milk just before serving. Hot or cold, garnish with a tiny dash of ground nutmeg.

●●●●

> Discover nonfat dry milk when fresh milk supplies run low. The secret to reconstituting it is to allow at least 2– 3 hours in the refrigerator, not only to chill it but to allow time for reluctant proteins to react fully with the water.

Posset

Far from home and feeling poorly? Here's a posset like Grandmother used to make. It will transport you back to the comforts of loved ones and home.

1 c. milk
2 t. sugar
Few grains salt
Few drops almond flavoring

Heat the milk to steaming, remove from heat, and stir in the salt and sugar until they dissolve. Add the almond extract, stir, and serve hot.

Variation: Use vanilla extract, or a drop of vanilla and a drop of almond.

●●●●

Slush

1 bag crushed ice
Powdered drink mix
Fresh strawberries for garnish

This makes a fun and attractive dessert after a big meal, and it can be made with sugared or unsugared drink mix. Send a team to the camp store for a bag of crushed ice and knock it around a bit to loosen it. Pack super-size glasses or paper cups with ice. Make up the powdered drink mix using only half as much water as it calls for and pour it over the ice. Serve with straws.

●●●●

> To make crushed ice, put cubes in a clean pillowcase and
> pound with a hammer.

Turkish Buttermilk

If you like the taste of buttermilk, you'll like this icy and energizing bracer.

1 pt. nonfat plain yogurt
2 c. water
Garlic salt to taste

Whisk everything together in a pitcher and chill thoroughly. Shake or stir again before serving.

●●●●

Your Own Chocolate Malt Mix

1 c. sugar or equivalent in sugar substitute
½ c. finest cocoa
Dash salt
⅓ c. cold water
½ c. malted milk

Make a smooth paste of all the ingredients and bring to a boil in a heavy saucepan over very low flame, or in the microwave. Take care not to burn it. Cool, and keep in the refrigerator. To prepare, add a teaspoon or two of the mixture to each cup of hot milk.

●●●●

Other Beverage Ideas

•Carry a few airline-size liqueurs in your favorite brand, and add half a bottle to each mug of coffee for a sweet, satisfying, easy dessert.

•For a change, use mulling spices with cranberry or pineapple juice instead of apple juice or cider. Serve hot, in mugs.

CHAPTER FOUR

Wake-up Call: Breakfast

At home, even with the help of countertop appliances, it's quite a juggling act to get the toast, bacon, eggs, and coffee hot and ready at the same time. In the RV galley, with too few burners and perhaps no appliances at all, it's even tougher. Here are some recipes that depart from the toast-eggs-bacon habit, to make cooking easier and tasting more of an adventure.

Breakfast Bread Pudding

½ loaf raisin bread
2 c. milk
3 eggs
Dash nutmeg
½ t. cinnamon
½ t. vanilla
Vanilla or lemon yogurt (optional)

Dice the bread and scatter it in a cold, buttered, heavy skillet. Whisk together the remaining ingredients, pour them over the bread, lid tightly, and bake over a low flame until the custard is set. Spoon into bowls and sauce with yogurt. Serves 4–6.

●●●●

Egg Mound Berry College

When we visited beautiful Berry College in the Georgia hills, this unusual egg dish was served. It's rich, eye-appealing, and ideal to make ahead of time. It keeps in the refrigerator for several days. For a quick breakfast on the go, serve it in individual disposable plastic drinking cups.

Hardboiled eggs, 1–2 per person
Curry powder to taste
Melted butter as needed for binding
Sour cream or plain yogurt

Mash the eggs and combine with a drizzle of melted butter to form a smooth paste. Be conservative with the butter so you don't pile on too many calories and a greasy taste. Then add curry powder to taste. Spoon into individual serving containers of ⅓ to ½ cup each, and frost with sour cream. Chill. This is eaten cold, with a spoon. It can also be served ice cream style, in flat-bottom ice cream cones. Fill, frost, and serve at once. Serve with a hot fruit compote, sweet rolls, and raspberry tea.

●●●●

Hardboiled eggs are the handiest of quick breakfasts. Keep a big supply on hand. Eat them cold, in casseroles, or add white sauce and a pinch of curry powder to make creamed eggs to serve over toast. To reduce total cholesterol, use a mixture of half mashed eggs, half mashed tofu.

Fried Cornmeal Mush

Once a country breakfast staple, fried mush is rarely found on today's tables and more rarely still in restaurants. It's a penny-pincher food, and a boon to the RV cook because it can be made ahead of time. Make up several bricks of mush at home, then slice off as much as you need each day.

1 c. yellow cornmeal
1 c. cold water
1 t. salt
3 c. boiling water

Mix the cornmeal, salt, and cold water in a saucepan. Then, stirring constantly over a low flame, stir in the boiling water. Cover and cook over very low heat or in a double boiler, stirring occasionally, for 30 minutes. Pour into an oiled loaf pan and chill. Slice ½ inch thick, dip in flour, and fry in butter until brown and crusty. Serve with syrup.

Variation: before chilling, stir in a pound of bulk sausage that has been fried out, drained well, and crumbled.

●●●●

Spoonbread with Bran

This is another cornmeal staple that combines the filling richness of eggs and milk with hearty cornmeal. Note that this is a three-step process involving extra dishwashing and stovetop cooking plus baking, but you may find, as I do, that it's worth the work. Send the family out on an early-morning birdwatching expedition while you boil and bake this.

2 c. milk
⅔ c. yellow cornmeal
¼ c. wheat bran or wheat germ
2 T. butter
¼ c. sugar
4 eggs, separated
½ t. salt
Toppings

Combine the milk, butter, sugar, salt, bran, and corn-meal in a medium saucepan and bring to a boil, stirring constantly. Cook, stirring, until it's thick and smooth, then stir in the egg yolks one at a time until well blended. Whisk the egg whites until they hold soft peaks and fold gently into the hot mixture. Immediately turn into a buttered 1½-quart casserole, and bake about 30 minutes at 350° until it's "set," as for custard. Serves 2–4. It's traditionally served with a pitcher of melted butter, but try it with fruit sauces, maple syrup, vanilla yogurt, and other toppings too.

••••

Birds Nest Brunch

1 pkg. brown rice and wild rice mix
8 eggs
4 oz. Swiss cheese, grated
8 oz. cooked smoky sausage
Small can evaporated milk
Canned French fried onion rings

Make up the rice mix according to package directions, spread in a buttered 9 X 13-inch pan or baking dish and make 8 indentations with the back of a big spoon. Into each, break an egg. Slice sausage thinly and arrange around eggs, then smother with grated cheese. Pour the milk over all. Sprinkle with French fried onion rings and bake in a 350° oven just until the dish is heated through and the eggs are set to your liking. Serves 4, with 2 eggs per person. This goes well with streusel coffee cake.

••••

Mexican Egg Casserole

6 corn tortillas
Oil
Small onion, chopped
1 clove garlic, mashed
2 T. cooked, crumbled bacon
8-oz. can stewed tomatoes
10-oz. pkg. frozen chopped spinach, thawed and drained well
8 hardboiled eggs, halved
8-oz. can or jar Mexican green sauce
4 oz. Monterey Jack cheese, grated

Sizzle the tortillas in a little oil until crisp, then drain and cut into noodle-size strips. Scatter in the bottom of a greased 8-inch square pan. Saute the onion and garlic in a little oil, then add the bacon and tomatoes. Stir in spinach and spread the mixture over the tortillas. Arrange the egg halves, yolk up, on this sauce. Pour green sauce over eggs, then sprinkle with grated cheese. Bake 15 minutes at 400°. This is a good choice to assemble ahead at home and bake aboard. Baking time will be a few minutes longer if the casserole has been refrigerated. If you want to add a bread course, stir up a boxed cornbread mix to bake with the casserole.

••••

Buy cooked, crumbled bacon, sold in supermarkets in cans and jars. A little goes a long way in flavoring breakfast eggs or breads, and it's much better than imitation bacon bits.

Breakfast Quiche

1 pkg. refrigerator crescent rolls
8-oz. pkg. pre-browned sausage
8-oz. pkg. grated cheese
6 eggs
½ c. milk

Unroll crescent rolls and press into a greased 9 X 13-inch baking pan. Bake 5 minutes at 375°. Cut up sausage and strew it and the grated cheese over the crust. Beat or shake eggs and milk together and pour over crust. Bake 30–35 minutes, or until set, at 350°. Let stand 5 minutes before cutting into squares. Serves 4.

●●●●

Apple-Topped Pancakes

Your favorite pancakes
1 c. maple-flavored syrup
¼ c. raisins
Dash cinnamon
1 can pie-sliced apples (not pie filling)
Vanilla yogurt

Heat together the syrup, raisins, and cinnamon with the undrained apples. When heated through, ladle over 4 big stacks of pancakes, and top each with a dollop of vanilla yogurt. Serves 4. Add crisp bacon and mugs of apple cinnamon tea.

●●●●

Rediscover creamed chipped beef on toast. For a shortcut, serve it over Holland rusk.

Add buttery color and taste to pancake or waffle batter by adding a jar of babyfood strained carrots or squash.

Sun's Up Cheesecake

If you have one of these creamy cheesecakes in the refrigerator, you can get an early start on a hot summer day. To add fiber to the meal, serve bran muffins or a bowl of bran cereal. Although it will look more like a cheesecake if it's baked in a spring-form pan, it's easier to bake and carry in a deep-dish pie plate.

1 c. graham cracker crumbs
½ stick butter, melted
3 eggs
12-oz. container cottage cheese
½ c. sugar
¼ t. salt
¼ t. cinnamon
½ t. vanilla
16-oz. container sour cream or yogurt
Orange marmalade

Mix the crumbs and melted butter and press them into a baking pan. Bake 10 minutes at 350°. Whisk together all the other ingredients except the marmalade, pour into the crust, and bake 30 minutes or until a knife blade put into the filling near the center comes out clean. Dot with orange marmalade, return to the oven for 5 minutes more, then spread the warmed marmalade evenly. Cool, then chill.

●●●●

Corned Beef Hashburgers

On a morning when you want to get an early start, serve these with crisp apples and cartons of juice for a complete drive-away breakfast you can eat with your hands, with no dishes to wash.

4 big hamburger buns
Butter
15-oz. can corned beef hash
4 slices pineapple

Lightly butter the buns and fry them, butter side down, in a nonstick skillet until toasty. Set aside. Remove both top and bottom of the hash can, push out the hash, and slice it into four pieces. Fry them in a lightly oiled non-stick skillet until they're crusty on both sides, topping each with a slice of pineapple for the last few minutes of cooking. Place each pineapple-hash stack in a hot bun. A quicker version, although it isn't as good, is to put the sliced hash and pineapple into the unbuttered buns, wrap each individually, and microwave on High for 30–45 seconds each.

●●●●

Breakfast Berries

Ah, the riches of RV travel! I'll never forget the raspberries we found during a trip to New Brunswick, the acres of wild blueberries in Ontario, the juicy sweetness of strawberries at a U-pick farm in Florida, and the wild blackberries, called brambles, we found during an RV trip through England.

1 stick butter or oleo	¾ c. rolled oats
¾ c. brown sugar	4 c. berries
½ c. flour	½ c. sugar
½ t. salt	1 T. cornstarch
½ t. cinnamon	2 T. cold water

Set out the butter until it reaches room temperature. Using a pastry cutter, or two knives held scissors style, cut the butter into the flour, brown sugar, oats, salt, and cinnamon. Set aside. (This can be done the night before.) Put the berries into a buttered 9-inch square pan, sprinkle with the sugar, and drizzle with a mixture of the cornstarch and water. Pile lightly (don't pack it down) with the oats mixture and bake at 350° about 40 minutes or until it's browned and bubbly. Serve warm in bowls, with light cream if you like.

●●●●

Applesauce Muffins

2 c. biscuit mix
1 egg, beaten
¼ c. sugar
2 T. oil
1 t. apple pie spice
8-oz. jar strained babyfood applesauce
⅓ c. milk
⅓ c. sugar
½ t. cinnamon
3 T. butter, melted

Combine the biscuit mix with the ¼ cup sugar and pie spice. Beat or shake together the egg, oil, applesauce, and milk. Combine wet and dry ingredients just until evenly mixed and spoon into 12 greased muffin tins. Bake about 12 minutes at 400°, cool for a few minutes, remove from pans, and dip tops in the melted butter, then into a mixture of the sugar and cinnamon. Serve with a ham omelet.

●●●●

Substitute paper-thin slices of smoked salmon for the Canadian bacon when making Eggs Benedict. Use Hollandaise sauce from a package mix.

Pineapple Dumplings

20-oz. can pineapple, in juice
1½ c. orange juice
2 c. biscuit mix
½ t. cinnamon
⅓ c. sugar
Milk

Combine the pineapple and juice in a large skillet and bring to a boil. Add the sugar and cinnamon to the biscuit mix, then add enough milk to make a stiff dough, stirring only enough to moisten evenly. Drop it by teaspoons atop the boiling fruit and keep at a simmer for 10 minutes, uncovered. Add more juice if needed. Cover, reduce heat, and simmer 10 minutes more. Serve at once, in bowls. Serves 4.

●●●●

Rosy Fruit Coffee Cake

Because this is a coarse-textured cake, you don't have to use an electric mixer or beat it for hours by hand. Serve it in warm, fragrant squares alone with coffee, or with scrambled eggs.

1 can condensed tomato soup
2 eggs
8-oz. can crushed pineapple
18-oz. package yellow cake mix
⅓ c. raisins
⅓ c. chopped nuts
2 c. grated coconut
½ stick butter
½ c. flour
⅓ c. brown sugar, packed

Combine the soup, eggs, and pineapple with its juice in a 9 X 13-inch pan and mix thoroughly. Stir in the cake mix, raisins, nuts, and 1½ cups of the coconut. Cut together the butter, brown sugar, flour, and remaining coconut, and sprinkle over the batter. Bake at 350° for 45–50 minutes or until it tests done with a toothpick. As a variation, try this with spice cake mix.

••••

Rainbow Dawn Dump Cake

As its name suggests, this dumps together and is baked and mixed right in the pan. It makes a moist, very sweet breakfast bread.

1 c. flour
1 c. sugar
½ t. cinnamon
½ c. shredded bran cereal
¾ t. baking soda
1 egg
Splash vanilla
8-oz. can fruit cocktail
Canned vanilla pudding, applesauce, or lemon yogurt

Mix the dry ingredients in an 8-inch baking pan and mix in the egg, vanilla, and fruit cocktail with its juice. Bake 30 minutes at 350°. Spoon into bowls and sauce with vanilla pudding, applesauce, or lemon yogurt.

••••

> Spoon canned tapioca pudding into serving dishes, top with well-drained peach slices, and sprinkle with All Bran or wheat germ for a sweet breakfast with texture contrast.

200-Mile Pancakes

These hearty, grainy pancakes are guaranteed to get you through the first 200 miles without the hungries, even though they contain no egg or fat. For an earlier getaway, mix up the dry ingredients the night before. Although it takes time to add all the different grains, they're the key to the rib-sticking richness of these flapjacks.

1 c. self-rising flour
½ t. baking soda
4 heaping T. any combination oatmeal, cornmeal, oat bran, wheat bran, wheat germ
1½ c. buttermilk or sour milk

Combine the dry ingredients, then mix in the milk just until everything is evenly moistened. Add a little more milk to make a thinner batter if you like. Spoon onto a hot greased or seasoned griddle and cook until browned on both sides. Serve your favorite way, with butter and syrup, sausage gravy, or fruit topping. Serves 2–3.

●●●●

Breakfast Baba

Inspired by a classic dessert, baba au rhum, this is made the night before and served at room temperature for a quick breakfast.

1 unflavored 9-inch baked pizza dough from the supermarket
1 c. sugar
1 c. strong tea
2 t. rum flavoring
1 can apricot pastry filling

Place the pizza dough in a cake or pie pan that it fits into well. Boil the sugar and tea 5 minutes, cool, mix in rum flavoring, and pour slowly over the pizza shell. When it has soaked in, spread with the apricot filling. Cover with plastic wrap and let stand overnight. Baba should be moist and sticky. Cut into wedges and serve.

●●●●

Hobo Breakfast

For this one, you'll need one clean 12- to 16-ounce tin can per serving. In the RV life, it doesn't take long to save up enough cans to make a batch of these all-in-one breakfasts to eat on the go. Once baked, they'll keep several days in the refrigerator, so you can grab them as needed.

Frozen bread dough
Hardboiled eggs
Real bacon bits
Squeeze margarine

Grease tin cans using a spray-on coating. Cut the frozen dough into 1-inch-thick slices. Press a slice of dough in the bottom of each can, sprinkle lightly with bacon bits, top with a peeled hardboiled egg, sprinkle with a little more bacon, and top with another chunk of dough, pressing it firmly over the egg. Drizzle with margarine. The can should be only half full.

Let rise just until the dough reaches the top of the can, (it will rise further; don't place it too close to the top of the oven), then bake at 350° until the dough is golden brown. Let cool slightly. If bread doesn't lift easily out of the can, remove the can bottom with a can opener and push it through. Serve in a paper napkin. Eat warm or cold, alone, or with butter and jam.

●●●●

Fanciful French Toast

Bread
1 jar mincemeat
Eggs
Milk
Rum (optional)
Butter for frying
Syrup or powdered sugar

Spread mincemeat on the bread to make one or two sandwiches per person. Whisk together eggs and milk, and a splash of rum if you like, as for French toast. Dip sandwiches in the mixture. Coat well but do not soak. Fry sandwiches in butter until brown and toasty on each side. Serve with maple syrup or sprinkle with powdered sugar.

Variations: Make the sandwiches with your favorite jam, peanut butter and jelly, peanut butter and real bacon bits, or mashed bananas. Turned into French toast, the sandwiches take on new heartiness, taste, and aroma. For a less sweet effect, make the sandwiches with cheese, egg salad, or bacon and tomato. Complement the flavors with white sauce, dill sauce, Hollandaise, or a tangy tomato salsa.

●●●●

Haystacks

½ c. crushed shredded wheat cereal
3 T. melted butter
4 T. brown sugar
3 T. chopped nuts
3 T. flaked coconut
Dash cinnamon
6 peach or pear halves

breakfast

Mix all ingredients except the fruit. Arrange the drained fruit, cut side up, in a buttered casserole or individual ramekins and fill centers with "haystacks" of the wheat mixture. Bake at 425° until the top is lightly browned and the fruit is well heated. Makes 6 portions to serve as a breakfast fruit or as a light main dish.

●●●●

Upset Applecart

Half stick butter or oleo
8-oz. can applesauce
¼ c. each raisins, chopped nuts, brown sugar
½ t. apple pie spice
Pkg. (10) refrigerator biscuits

Melt the butter in a deep pie pan in a 425° oven, turning the pan so it is well coated. Stir in the remaining ingredients except biscuits and return to the oven for 3–5 minutes. Top the hot mixture with the biscuits and return to oven for 15 minutes or until the biscuits are golden brown. Working carefully and wearing thick oven mitts (the apple mixture will be boiling hot), place a serving plate over the pie dish and flip over. Serve at once as a breakfast main course, or as a coffee cake with a ham omelette.

To double this recipe, use a 9 X 13-inch pan, but don't attempt to flip it. Serve it with a spoon, sauce side up.

●●●●

To add fiber to breakfast, stir 1 t. miller's bran into each carton of fruited yogurt. Eat it alone, or use it as a spread for toast or muffins.

Openface Sunup Sandwich

6 thick slices hearty bread, buttered
3-oz. pkg. cream cheese, at room temperature
Cinnamon sugar
6 t. real bacon bits
6 pear halves, sliced
6 thin slices Swiss or Jarlsberg cheese

Arrange the bread, butter side down, on a lightly greased baking sheet. Spread the bread thinly with cream cheese and sprinkle very lightly with cinnamon sugar. Sprinkle with real bacon bits, then cover with a layer of thinly sliced fresh or well-drained canned pears. Bake 5 minutes at 350°, place a slice of cheese on each, and return to the oven until the bread is toasty on the bottom and the cheese has melted over the pears. Makes 6; plan 2–3 per person for hearty eaters.

••••

New Orleans Breakfast Puffs (Calas)

Make the dough the night before. On a morning when you have time to fuss a bit, fry these puffs to golden perfection and send out a scent that will bring the crew out of the woods in a hurry. They're an ideal way to use left-over rice.

2 c. cooked rice
2 c. biscuit mix
2 T. sugar
1½ t. apple pie spice
2 eggs
½ c. milk
1 t. vanilla
Oil for frying

Put the dry ingredients in a roomy bowl. Whisk or shake together the wet ingredients and stir into the dry ingredients just until well moistened. Cover and refrigerate overnight. Heat about 2 inches of oil in a roomy, deep skillet to 400°. Calas will be soggy if the fat is not hot enough. As a test, drop in a small cube of white bread, which should brown in 50 seconds. Drop the cold batter by tablespoons into the hot oil and brown them on one side, then turn and brown the other. Remove the hot calas to a bowl lined with paper towel and drizzle with a glaze made from:

1 c. powdered sugar
½ t. vanilla
Water to make a thin frosting (1–2 T.)

●●●●

Cajun Huevos Rancheros (Mexican eggs with a Creole accent)

One of my favorite quips about the harmonious melting pot that is America, is about the Mexican restaurant that serves pizza because it's in a Jewish neighborhood. That story may not be true, but I do know of a Chinese restaurant in Miami that serves Cuban black beans and rice and a Cuban restaurant that serves turkey and stuffing every day. Here is another only-in-America blend of ethnic tastes.

4 c. cooked grits
8 oz. smoked sausage
2 T. grated cheese
2 T. butter
Seasoned flour or breadcrumbs
Fried or poached eggs
Creole tomato sauce
Shredded jack cheese (optional)

Stir the finely cut-up sausage, cheese, and butter into the hot grits and spread in a buttered jellyroll pan. Cover with waxed paper and chill overnight. Cut into squares. All this can be done at home if you like. Stack the squares, separated by bits of waxed paper, in plastic bags and store them in the refrigerator. To assemble the dish, dip each square of the cold grits in seasoned flour or bread crumbs and fry in butter until brown and toasty. Top each with a fried or poached egg and top with hot Creole tomato sauce—your own favorite recipe or one from a can or jar. Top with a tuft of grated cheese for added richness.

●●●●

Stuffed Ham Omelet

1½ cups cold stuffing
4 slices deli baked ham
2 T. butter
8 eggs
½ c. milk

Use leftover stuffing or add hot water to a mix to make 1½ cups. Form the stuffing into 4 sausage-shaped cylinders and roll up each one in a slice of ham. Melt the butter in a 10-inch nonstick skillet. Add ham rolls, seam side down, in 4 "spokes." Mix the eggs and milk, pour over ham, cover, and cook over medium heat until eggs are just set. Uncover and let stand 5 minutes. Using a utensil that is safe for nonstick coatings, cut the omelet into 4 portions with a ham roll in the center of each and place on plates.

●●●●

Bread: A Lust for Loafing

As You Like It Loaf

This versatile loaf can be made with many variations. Use what you have on hand, including lots of imagination and daring.

3 c. flour (may include up to
  ½ c. whole wheat flour,
  cornmeal, or oatmeal)
2 t. baking powder
½ t. baking soda
½ t. salt
1 t. apple pie spice
1 egg
¼ c. oil
½ c. light molasses, corn
  syrup, or maple syrup
¾ c. buttermilk, sour milk, or
  yogurt thinned with a little milk

Plus
1 c. grated carrots, pineapple,
  or apples
Or 1 c. mashed pumpkin,
  bananas, or sweet potatoes
Or ½ c. finely chopped cran-
  berries
Or 1 c. fresh blueberries, raspberries, or strawberries

Plus
½ c. raisins (optional)
½ c. chopped nuts (optional)

41

Grease a loaf pan. Mix the dry ingredients in a large bowl and make a well in the center. Whisk together the egg, sweetener, oil, and milk and add all at once to the dry ingredients. Mix just until everything is evenly moistened. Quickly fold in the fruit of your choice, and any nuts and raisins. Pour into the pan and bake at 350° for about 60 minutes or until the bread tests done with a toothpick. Let stand 15 minutes in the pan. Turn out onto a rack. Cool, then slice with a serrated knife. These breads slice easier if wrapped and stored overnight.

●●●●

Easy Cheesy Danish

Pkg. (about 12) brown-and-serve rolls
3-oz. pkg. cream cheese
1 egg
3 T. sugar
1 T. lemon juice

Heat the oven to 400°. Let the cream cheese come to room temperature. Arrange rolls, packed tightly together, in a greased pan and, using the handle of a wooden spoon, poke three or four holes in each roll almost all the way to the bottom. Beat the other ingredients together and carefully pour into the holes in the rolls. Bake until rolls are browned and cheese mixture has set.

●●●●

Keep canned breads on hand for emergencies and unexpected guests. They include canned corn tortillas, Boston brown bread, canned specialty breads sold in gourmet shops, and crackers packed, export-style, in tins.

> Quick breads cut easiest if they have been tightly wrapped and
> held overnight. However, they are hard to resist when fresh
> and hot. A serrated bread knife will do the best cutting job.

Microwave Health Bread

*Throw this together in seconds and bake it in mere minutes. It can be
baked in any suitable container, such as a bake-proof measuring cup or in a
wide-mouth, pint-size canning jar. The bread will be firmer and slice more
easily if you cool it first.*

1 c. whole wheat flour
½ c. cornmeal
1 t. baking soda
1 c. buttermilk, sour milk, or thin yogurt
⅓ c. molasses
½ c. raisins
½ c. chopped nuts

Combine dry ingredients except raisins and nuts. Add
wet ingredients. Stir just until evenly moistened, then
fold in raisins and nuts. Pour half into a greased one-
pint, microwave-safe container, cover loosely with wrap,
and microwave on Medium 5–7 minutes, rotating every
few minutes, until firm around the edges. Let stand 5
minutes before turning out. Repeat with other half of
dough. Slice and serve with a fancy butter.

●●●●

The Best Bran Muffins

*Everyone is baking bran muffins these days. I keep coming back to this
recipe for taste, for high fiber and low fat content, and for cost savings because*

it uses bran and not an expensive bran cereal. If your supermarket doesn't sell plain miller's bran, find it at health-food stores.

2 c. flour
1½ c. miller's bran
½ t. salt
1½ t. soda
2 c. buttermilk or thin yogurt
½ c. molasses
¼ c. oil
½ c. raisins
1 T. grated fresh orange rind if you have some

Mix all dry ingredients (the night before if you like). Dump in the liquids, mix just to moisten evenly, and fold in raisins. Fill greased muffin cups ⅔ full and bake 15–20 minutes at 425°. Makes 24 muffins.

●●●●

Butterscotch Pecan Rolls

1 package (12) brown-and-serve rolls
1 butterscotch pudding mix (not instant)
6-oz. package pecan pieces

Line muffin pan with cupcake papers, place a roll in each, and bake according to manufacturer's directions. Meanwhile, prepare the pudding mix according to package directions and fold in broken pecans. Using an ice pick, puncture the hot rolls several times at varying depths and pour in the hot pudding mix. Cool for a few minutes without removing the rolls from the pan, then remove to serving plates. Gooey and good!

●●●●

Spicy Carrot Loaf

2¼ c. flour	1 t. apple pie spice
1⅓ c. uncooked oatmeal	⅓ c. salad oil
¾ c. dark brown sugar, packed	¾ c. water
½ c. raisins	2 eggs
4 t. baking powder	2 jars (4½ oz. each) babyfood
½ t. baking soda	strained carrots
Dash salt	

Combine dry ingredients and mix well. Combine wet ingredients. Add wet ingredients to dry and mix only until evenly moistened. Spread in a greased 9 X 5-inch loaf pan and bake at 350° for 70–75 minutes. Test for doneness. Let stand 10–15 minutes, then turn out.

●●●●

Quick Cinnammmmmuffins

1 c. butter
8-oz. carton sour cream
2 c. self-rising flour
Cinnamon sugar

Let the butter come to room temperature or soften it in the microwave oven. Whisk together butter and sour cream and stir in self-rising flour just until blended. Sprinkle with cinnamon sugar. Fill paper-lined muffin pans ⅔ full and bake 25–30 minutes at 350°. These are so rich and buttery, they don't really need additional butter. Serve them plain or with strawberry jam.

●●●●

Tin Can Breads

Remove the tops of fruit and vegetable tins carefully, leaving a clean rim. Rinse and dry the tins and save four or five for this recipe. You'll have no loaf pans to wash.

2 c. sugar	4 eggs
2 t. salt	1 c. oil
4 c. flour	2 c. mashed pumpkin or bananas
1 T. apple pie spice	⅔ c. milk
1 t. baking powder	**Optional:** ½ c. nuts, ½ c. raisins
2 t. baking soda	

Combine the dry ingredients in a plastic bag and shake to mix. In a roomy bowl whisk together the wet ingredients and add the dry ingredients all at once. Mix only to moisten evenly, then fold in the nuts and raisins. Fill greased tin cans half full and bake at 350° until the loaves test done (a toothpick plunged into the center will come out clean). Let cool completely and wrap. To serve, remove can bottoms with a can opener and push out the bread. Slice into rounds. This bread toasts deliciously. Butter slices lightly and fry them in a nonstick skillet until they are brown and crusty.

●●●●

South in Yo' Mouth Biscuits

The secret to making real buttermilk biscuits, Southern style, is to use all-vegetable white shortening and the soft wheat flour sold in the South under such brand names as Martha White and White Lily.

2 c. self-rising flour, Southern regional brand
Pinch baking powder
1 T. sugar
¾ c. shortening
1 c. buttermilk

Mix the dry ingredients and cut in the shortening with a pastry blender or two knives until the mixture is filled with lumps about the size of peas. Stir in the buttermilk and turn out dough onto a well-floured dishtowel. Knead lightly, 4–5 times, and pat into a ¾-inch circle. Cut into rounds and bake 10–12 minutes at 425°. Serve hot.

●●●●

Your Own Bread Sticks

Day-old hot dog buns
1 stick butter
Poppy seeds, toasted sesame seeds, or grated hard cheese

Slice each bun into 6 strips, dip lightly in melted butter, and dip in seeds or cheese. Bake on a cookie sheet at 350° about 15 minutes or until golden.

●●●●

Corny Bread

½ stick butter
3 c. biscuit mix
2 eggs
1 pint sour cream
1-lb. can cream-style corn
8 oz. cheddar cheese, grated
½ t. paprika

Melt the butter in a 9 X 13-inch pan and tilt to coat the pan well. Put the biscuit mix in a large bowl. Whisk together the eggs, sour cream, cheese, corn, and paprika, and mix with the biscuit mix just until everything is well moistened. Bake at 425° about 30 minutes or until it's lightly browned around the edges and springy in the middle.

Variation: Add 2 c. sautéed onions, cooled, with the corn mixture.

●●●●

Scones, Master Recipe

To make your own scone ready-mix, multiply the dry ingredients by as many times as you wish. Keep tightly covered in a cool place. For each batch of 8 scones, add 1 egg, ¼ cup butter, and ⅔ cup buttermilk to 2¼ cups dry mix.

2 c. flour
2 T. sugar
2 t. baking powder
½ t. soda
½ t. salt
¼ c. cold butter
⅔ c. buttermilk or sour milk
1 egg

Combine the dry ingredients. Cut the butter into pieces. Now cut the butter into the dry ingredients with two knives or a pastry blender. (British cooks do it with their fingers, using a quick, light, pinching motion.) Beat the egg and milk together and mix in quickly. Knead on a floured paper towel 5–6 times, just to mix well. Unlike yeast breads, which improve with kneading, quick breads need a light touch. Pat the ball of dough into an 8-inch circle on a greased baking sheet and score it into 8 wedges. Do not cut through. Bake about 15 minutes at 425°, or until golden. Cut into wedges and serve warm with butter and jam.

To make your own economical biscuit mix, cut 4 c. regular or butter-flavored shortening into 16 c. self-rising flour. Keep tightly lidded in a cool place.

Variations:

•For a Scottish touch, substitute brown sugar for white, and substitute ¼ c. raw oatmeal for ¼ c. of the flour. Sprinkle with another ¼ c. oats before scoring dough.

And additions (to mix in after cutting in butter):

•For a Mexican touch, ½ c. Mexicorn.

•To make a simple scone-and-salad lunch, ½ c. freshly grated cheese; serve with green salad vinaigrette.

•For breakfast, ½ c. cut-up dried prunes or apricots and ¼ c. chopped walnuts.

•To accompany a scrambled eggs breakfast, 2 T. real bacon bits.

Yeast Bread

Most of us don't take time during RV travels to make traditional loaves. Still, there's no real substitute for yeast bread, so I keep on hand a box of hot roll mix, a tube of refrigerated bread dough, or a loaf or two of frozen bread dough, which can be raised and baked when needed. Here's a quick compromise that reduces the time and steps needed to make a yeast loaf from scratch. It needs little kneading. Note that it calls for self-rising flour, which makes it twice as fast and twice as foolproof.

1 pkg. yeast
1 stick butter, melted
½ c. warm water
¼ c. sugar
2 eggs, beaten
6–7 c. self-rising flour
1½ c. warm milk

In a large bowl, sprinkle the yeast over the water to dissolve it, then stir in the remaining ingredients, adding flour as needed to make a stiff dough. Cover the bowl with a clean towel and let it stand in a warm place, away from any wind, until it's doubled in bulk. Turn out onto a clean, floured dishtowel and knead in more flour as necessary to make the dough easy to handle. Divide in half, shape into two loaves, place in greased loaf pans, and let rise until double in bulk. Bake at 400° until the loaves are golden brown and sound hollow when tapped.

●●●●

Blue Corn Muffins

Once available only in the Southwest, blue cornmeal is now found in specialty shops nationwide. Look for it in your travels. It's a staple in Tex-Mex cooking, and you'll find many recipes that call for it. Here is one way to enjoy it.

1½ c. blue cornmeal	2 eggs
1 c. flour	1½ c. milk
⅓ c. sugar	¾ c. margarine, melted
1 T. baking powder	8-oz. can Mexicorn
1 t. salt	

Combine the dry ingredients in a bowl. Beat or shake together the eggs and milk, and stir into the dry ingredients just to moisten. Fold in the melted margarine and the Mexicorn and fill 24 muffin cups ⅔ to ¾ full. Bake at 350° 20–25 minutes or until the muffins are springy to the touch. If you don't have muffin pans aboard, bake this as for cornbread in a greased pan or casserole.

●●●●

For easier mixing of the wet ingredients for a quick bread, shake them up in a tightly lidded container (such as a juice bottle), preferably one you're about to throw away.

Porridge Muffins

1⅔ c. flour
2 T. brown sugar
2 t. baking powder
Dash salt
1½ c. milk
1 c. cooked oatmeal
2 eggs
1 T. olive oil

Combine the dry ingredients in a bowl. Beat together the wet ingredients, pour into the dry, and mix just until everything is moistened evenly. Bake in well-greased muffin tins about 20–25 minutes at 425°. Let stand a few minutes before turning out of the pan.

●●●●

Gingerbread

Think of this gingerbread as a bread, not as a dessert. It's a zesty companion for a meal of baked ham and scalloped potatoes, or bratwurst with boiled and buttered potatoes.

2¼ c. flour
2 T. finely chopped candied ginger
1 t. ground ginger
1 t. baking soda
1 c. beer
½ c. oil
½ c. light molasses
1 egg, beaten

Stir together the dry ingredients in a bowl, then whisk together the wet ingredients and dump all at once into the dry. Mix just to moisten evenly and turn into a greased 9-inch square pan. Bake 45–50 minutes at 325°. Let cool 10 minutes before cutting into squares.

••••

Bran Muffins Jarlsberg

When we want to hit the road very early, I assemble the ingredients the night before, bake these while we're getting ready to roll, then serve them on the go with hot coffee. They are rich and moist enough to be eaten plain, without butter, and are hearty enough to constitute a real stick-to-the-ribs breakfast.

½ c. flour	1 c. milk
¼ c. miller's bran	Small apple, chopped
⅓ c. brown sugar	¼ c. oil
¼ c. chopped nuts	1 egg
¼ c. butter, softened	¾ c. shredded Jarlsberg cheese
16-oz. package date-bread mix	

In a small bowl mix the butter, flour, and sugar until crumbly. Set aside. In a large bowl combine remaining ingredients. Mix with a wooden spoon just until well blended with no dry particles. Spoon the mixture into paper-lined muffin cups, filling no more than ⅔ full, and sprinkle with the crumb mixture. Bake at 400° about 20 minutes or until they test done. Cool in the pan 5 minutes, then remove to cooking rack. Serve warm-m-m-m. This makes a dozen regular-size muffins.

••••

More About Beer Bread

To a teetotal family the taste and smell of beer are distasteful, but I urge everyone to discover the convenience and springy texture of beer bread. The alcohol cooks away, leaving a yeasty taste and a true bread-like consistency that slices, toasts, and makes sandwiches like no other quick bread.

The recipe for beer bread has been printed time and again, so it hardly needs repeating here except as a starting point for the variations I have developed. It is simply

12 oz. beer
3 c. self-rising flour
1 T. sugar

Pour the (room temperature) beer into a medium bowl, add the flour and sugar, and blend only until it is evenly moistened. Turn it into a greased bread pan or deep casserole and bake at 350° about 45 minutes or until it's brown and sounds hollow when tapped. Slice with a serrated bread knife. Like most breads, beer bread tastes best when it is hot but will be easier to slice thin and evenly for toast or sandwiches if it has been cooled, wrapped, and "seasoned" overnight.

Variations:

• Substitute up to 1 c. whole wheat, rye, soy, or oat flour for the self-rising flour. Always add 1½ t. baking powder and an extra pinch of salt when using a cup of non-self-rising flour.

• Substitute honey, molasses, or maple syrup for the sugar. To intensify maple flavor, add ½ t. maple extract.

• To make a fruit-nut loaf, add up to a cup of cut-up dried apricots, dates, candied cherries, raisins, chopped walnuts, pitted prunes, or the like.

• To create raisin bread, add 1 t. cinnamon and an extra 1 T. sugar, plus 1 c. raisins to the batter.

• When using part rye flour, add 1 T. grated orange rind or 1 T. caraway seeds.

• Invent an herb-cheese bread by adding 1 T. dried herbs and 2–3 T. grated hard cheese.

Soup's On

Soup is the essence of cold-weather comfort cuisine. Soups to sip from a mug or spoon from a bowl are among life's most intoxicating pleasures. Make a simple soup into a hearty meal by adding a salad and mountains of hot bread. Have it for lunch, for a snack, for a calmer at bedtime, and as a soothing healer of road-jangled nerves.

Most of these are shortcut soups, yet they have superb flavor and a touch of class.

Corn Chowder with Brie

6 oz. round Brie
Small onion, minced
2 T. butter
1-lb. can cream-style corn
12-oz. can chicken broth
1 can evaporated skim milk
¼ t. dried dill weed

Cut the Brie into 8 pieces and place 2 in each of 4 soup bowls. Let it come to room temperature. Sauté the onion in the butter until it's tender, then add the corn and chicken broth and bring to a boil for about 2 minutes. Remove from heat, add the milk and dill weed, and ladle immediately over the Brie. Serve with pilot crackers, sweet butter, and a fruity dessert such as blueberry buckle or apple betty.

●●●●

Seafood Bisque

1 can condensed cream of mushroom soup
1 can condensed tomato soup
1 soup-can water
1 can evaporated milk
6-oz. can shrimp or crab, drained and picked over
Sherry

Combine the soups, water, and milk in a saucepan and heat, stirring, over medium flame until smooth and well heated. Do not boil. Stir in seafood and continue heating. Ladle into bowls and add a splash of sherry to each. Serves 4.

●●●●

Golden Potato Soup

2 servings instant mashed potatoes
4½-oz. jar strained babyfood carrots
1 T. instant onion flakes
1 can condensed chicken broth
1 soup-can milk
Salt and pepper to taste
Fresh parsley

Make instant potatoes according to package directions for two servings. Stir in remaining ingredients and heat, stirring often, until thoroughly heated. Sprinkle with chopped parsley if you have some. Makes 4 small appetizers or 2 main-dish servings.

●●●●

Poached Egg Soup

This makes a light supper or a quick roadside lunch. For each two servings:

14-oz. can ready-to-serve chicken broth
¼ c. water
2 eggs
1 c. shredded lettuce
Grated Parmesan or Romano cheese

Heat the broth and water in a skillet and, using a spoon to make a whirlpool in the center, poach the eggs, one at a time, in the boiling liquid. As each egg is done, remove it to a soup bowl. Add the lettuce to the broth and cook just until it's wilted. Spoon broth over the eggs, sprinkle with cheese, and serve with buttered rusks.

●●●●

Chunky Chicken Clam Chowder

1 can cream of chicken soup
1 soup-can milk
10-oz. pkg. frozen mixed vegetables
Pinch dried thyme
2 cans, 5–6 oz. each, chunk chicken
6-oz. can clams, with juice
Butter

Mix everything but the butter in a roomy saucepan and simmer over low heat until the vegetables are tender. Set out 4 soup bowls and put a pat of butter in each. Add the soup. Serve with oyster crackers or big, buttery, homemade croutons.

●●●●

Pleasant Peasant Ragout

This is a very filling soup/stew to serve on a cold night. It is a good choice for preparation at home, to be warmed up on board in the microwave.

6 meaty, skinless chicken thighs	16-oz. can tomatoes
6 sweet Italian sausages	1 t. mixed Italian herbs
2 T. oil	Green pepper, diced
Lg. onion, diced	2-lb. can white kidney beans
2 cloves garlic, mashed	1 can condensed beef broth
	1 soup-can water, part red wine

Brown the chicken and sausage in hot oil in a roomy saucepan. Continue stirring and frying while sautéing the onion and garlic. Pour off excess fat. Add tomatoes, broth, wine, and herbs. Cover and simmer 15–20 minutes over low heat. Add beans and green pepper, cover, and simmer 10 minutes more. Spoon into soup plates. Serves 6.

Add a leafy salad and Boston brown bread from a can, buttered with whipped cream cheese. Give everyone a licorice whip to eat while you all wind up the evening with a brisk hike in the twilight.

> Toasted bread with a broiled-on cheese topping can be used as a hearty, meal-making topping on almost any hot soup, not just French onion. Float it atop bowls of minestrone, cream of potato, or cream of asparagus.

Rosy Glow Soup

1 can cream of mushroom soup
2 jars babyfood strained beets
1 soup-can milk
Sour cream (optional)

Whisk together soup, milk, and beets and heat thoroughly. Add a dollop of sour cream to each bowl if you like. Serves 2–3.

Variations: Stir in babyfood carrots, squash, or peas to create other cream soups. Add a dash of nutmeg or a dash of dried dill weed.

●●●●

Lightning Chowder

1 can cream of celery soup
1 can cream of potato soup
2 soup-cans milk
6½-oz. can tuna
4 pats butter
Approx. ½ t. dried thyme

Whisk together the soups and milk in a saucepan and stir in the tuna. Heat until steaming. Place a pat of butter in each soup bowl and sprinkle with thyme. Ladle soup over the butter. Serves 4.

●●●●

When making vegetable soup, use a medley of barley, rice, orzo, millet, broken spaghetti, and what have you, rather than just one starch.

Summer Soups To Serve Cold

Cold Bean-Tomato Soup

Make this ahead of time at home and chill for up to two days while flavors mingle and marry. Somewhat like gazpacho, this is hearty enough to serve as a main dish in hot weather.

16-oz. can tomatoes, with
 juice
16-oz. can tomato juice
19-oz. can white beans,
 drained
¼ bell pepper, minced
2 T. olive oil

1 T. lime juice
Small Bermuda onion,
 finely diced
¼ t. garlic salt
¼ t. onion salt
Dash Tabasco
1 c. fresh parsley, snipped

Coarsely chop tomatoes and place everything in a bowl. Lid tightly and chill thoroughly. Serves 3–4.

●●●●

Cucumber Soup

2 med. cucumbers
2 qts. buttermilk
1 t. dill weed
1 T. dried chopped chives
Salt, pepper to taste
¼ c. chopped fresh parsley

Peel and seed the cucumbers and chop finely. Mix all ingredients, adjust seasonings, and chill thoroughly. If you have fresh dill, use it generously instead of the dried. If you don't have fresh parsley, use none. Serves 6–8.

●●●●

Orange Soup

5 c. tomato juice or tomato
   juice cocktail
½ c. orange juice concentrate
2 T. lemon juice

2 T. sugar
Salt, pepper, garlic salt to taste
Thin slices lemon
Lemon yogurt (optional)

Mix all ingredients together and chill. Garnish each serving with a paper-thin slice of lemon. For a richer garnish, add a dollop of lemon yogurt.

●●●●

Avocado Soup

3 med. avocados, mashed to a smooth paste
2 T. lemon juice
2 c. plain nonfat yogurt
2 c. beef broth
Dash paprika
Onion salt to taste

Mash the avocado with the lemon juice, then gradually stir in the remaining ingredients. Chill. Serves 4–6.

●●●●

Jellied Soup

2 cans jellied consommé, chilled
2 T. lemon juice
2-oz. jar caviar
Small onion, minced
Sour cream

Slice consommé into serving-size rounds. Mix the caviar

with the lemon juice and scatter on the consommé. Sprinkle with minced onion and top with a dab of sour cream.

●●●●

––––––––––––––––

Mock Turtle Soup

Because this is such a thick and meaty soup, it makes a perfect main course when served with a salad and rolls. Its secret is a classic roux made with real butter and cooked to coppery perfection. It rewarms well in the microwave or in a double boiler, so it can be made at home and reheated on the first or second night out.

1 T. oil
1 T. butter
1½ lbs. ground turkey
Lg. onion, diced
2 ribs celery, diced
3 cloves garlic, minced
1 t. each ground cumin,
　thyme, oregano
3 lg. bay leaves

1-lb. can pureed tomatoes
4 c. water
4 t. beef bouillon granules
For the roux:
1 c. butter
¾ c. flour
For garnish:
Sherry
3–4 hardboiled eggs

In a roomy skillet or pot melt the tablespoon of butter with the oil and brown the turkey with the onion, celery, and garlic until the vegetables are just tender. Stir in the spices, whole bay leaves, tomatoes, water, and bouillon and simmer without covering about 45 minutes over very low flame. Stir occasionally.

Meanwhile, make the roux. In a heavy skillet melt the cup of butter, stir in the flour, and cook, stirring, over a medium flame for 20–25 minutes or until it's the color of a dark copper penny. Remove the bay leaves, stir the roux into the soup mixture, and cook, stirring, over medium heat until it's thick and hot. Ladle into soup bowls, splash with sherry if desired, and sprinkle with chopped hardboiled eggs. Makes 2 quarts of soup.

●●●●

Hurry-up Thuringer and Bean Soup

This soup gets off to a fast start because you begin with fully cooked meat and beans. If you don't have a blender or food processor aboard, mash the beans and cut up the onion and garlic for a slightly coarser and more robust soup. To serve a family of 4–5, double this recipe.

6 oz. cooked, smoked Thuringer links
16-oz. can Great Northern beans
Small onion, quartered
1 clove garlic, halved
1 c. beef broth
¼ c. dry sherry
¾ t. ground cumin
Green onion, chives, parsley (optional)

Place the beans, onion, and garlic in blender or food processor and grind until smooth. Add the broth, sherry, and cumin, and blend. Pour into a 2-quart microwave container, cover and vent, and cook on High 5 minutes. Or put the mixture in a saucepan, bring to a boil, reduce heat, cover, and simmer 10–15 minutes. Add the sausage, which has been cut into thin slices, and cook another 5–6 minutes to heat through. Garnish with onion, parsley, and chives if you like. Serves 2–3. This hearty, warming soup calls for slabs of bread torn from a fresh French loaf, an apple salad, and tin roof sundaes for dessert.

●●●●

Fast Lane

•Save a soy sauce bottle, the type with a plastic shaker insert, and fill it with sherry. Pass at the table to splash into soups and stews.

•To turn a thin soup into a hearty main dish, make up biscuit mix according to package directions and float small dumplings atop boiling soup. Boil 10 minutes uncovered, 10 minutes more covered. A cup of biscuit mix makes enough dumplings for each 3–4 cups soup.

•To enrich a thin soup, beat a couple of eggs and pour them in a thin stream into the boiling soup while stirring constantly.

•When you're out of evaporated milk for use in chowder, mix up a batch of nonfat dry milk double strength. Add an extra pat of butter.

•To make canned soups taste more like homemade, combine two or more flavors. Good combinations include cream of tomato with split pea, minestrone with bean, cream of potato with New England clam chowder, or cream of mushroom with broccoli cheese.

•Make your favorite oyster stew recipe using bay scallops instead and discover a new taste treat.

•To thicken any soup, stir in 1–2 T. oatmeal or potato flakes.

Anytime Foods: Sandwiches, Appetizers, Snacks

This is my collection of recipes for those times when you're on the go at odd hours and need a nosh.

Of all the foods we rely on in the gadabout life, cheese sandwiches lead the way. They can be crammed into a backpack, snuck into a movie or ball game, or nibbled while stuck in traffic or waiting in line.

They can be frozen for future use, cut into bite-size squares and served as cocktail snacks, or turned into a melty, hot meal by frying them in butter. (Dip cheese sandwiches into a mixture of egg and milk and fry as for French toast, and you have a feast.)

The secret is to use the best whole-grain breads and a good cheese, such as Vermont sharp cheddar. Butter the bread if you like, then paste liberally with a substantial mustard.

Anything else, such as sliced tomatoes, lettuce, meat, or mayonnaise should be added later, just before serving. If you confine the basic recipe to the bread, butter, mustard, and cheese, these sandwiches will keep several days without refrigeration or fear of spoilage.

> **Make your own cracker snacks. Place ready-made pie crust on a cookie sheet, score it very lightly into wedges, and sprinkle it with seasoned salt, sesame seeds, or poppy seeds. Bake at 400° until it's brown.**

Veggie Cheese Melt Sandwiches

12 oz. mushrooms, cleaned and sliced
¼ c. butter
2 c. sprouts and thinly sliced vegetables (sweet
peppers, zucchini, yellow squash, cabbage)
Lg. onion, sliced into rings
Soy sauce
16 oz. sharp cheddar cheese, grated
10 slices bread

Sauté the mushrooms in the melted butter in a large skillet, adding and stir-frying remaining vegetables over medium heat until everything is crisp-tender. Season with several splashes of soy sauce. Top five pieces of bread with some of the grated cheese, then well-drained hot vegetables, the remaining cheese, and another slice of bread. Cover with a clean dishtowel for a few minutes to allow the heat of the vegetables to melt the cheese, then cut sandwiches in half and serve.

●●●●

Passing Lane Sandwich Puffs

When you're out of bread, make elegant sandwiches by rustling up a batch of cream puffs.

1 stick butter or oleo
1 c. water
1 c. flour
4 eggs

Bring the butter and water to a boil and remove from heat. Dump in the flour all at once and mix. Continue mixing, adding the eggs one at a time, to make a thick dough. Drop by tablespoons onto a greased baking sheet and bake at 400° for 10 minutes, then 350° for about 25 minutes more. Dough should lose its shiny look and appear dry. Let cool in the oven with the door ajar. Fill with sandwich filling such as chicken, tuna, or ham salad.

Variations: Add a teaspoon of Dijon mustard and ½ cup grated cheese to the dough. Instead of forming individual puffs, dough can be spread in a circle or a ring. Cut in half horizontally, fill with sandwich makings, then slice into wedges. To make cocktail snacks, make smaller puffs by the teaspoon and stuff with your favorite filling.

●●●●

Battered Sandwich

This works best with sandwich fillings that hold together well with the bread, such as ham or chicken salad or a filling bound with grated cheese (which melts as it cooks, cementing the ingredients).

4 sandwiches
1 c. pancake mix
1 egg
1 c. milk
Oil for deep-frying

Cut sandwiches in half. Whisk together pancake mix, egg, and milk and dip the sandwich in the batter, coating it thoroughly. (If any of the filling is exposed, it may spit and spatter during cooking.) Heat an inch or two of oil in a roomy skillet and fry sandwiches until they are crispy and brown. Drain on paper towel. Careful when taking the first bite! The filling is sealed in, bursting with heat and steam.

●●●●

Pit-Stop Pasties

2 pkg. crescent rolls
4 oz. grated cheese
¾ lb. ham salad from the deli

Separate the rolls into triangles. Mix the ham salad with the grated cheese and divide among 8 of the triangles. Top carefully with the remaining dough. Seal each pasty (rhymes with nasty) by moistening edges with water. Then press securely. Bake on a greased cookie sheet in a 350° oven for 10–15 minutes or until golden and crusty.

●●●●

"Crab" Salad Pockets

8 oz. imitation crab meat
1 T. lemon juice
1 rib celery, diced
2–3 scallions, sliced
8-oz. can crushed pine-
   apple, well drained

¼ c. slivered almonds
Mayonnaise
½ t. curry powder
Avocado
4 pitas

Buy an imitation crab that is fully cooked and ready to eat, and shred or chop it in a small bowl. Splash with lemon juice. Add the celery, onions, pineapple, curry powder, and almonds, and enough mayonnaise to bind the mixture. Divide into pita bread halves and garnish each with a slice of ripe avocado.

●●●●

When you're out of celery add crunch to sandwich fillings by using diced canned water chestnuts or bamboo shoots, well drained.

Onion Pie

3 jumbo sweet onions
½ stick butter
9-inch unbaked pie shell
1 lb. cottage cheese
2 eggs
½ t. salt, dash each pepper and nutmeg

Slice the onions thinly and sauté in the butter until they are limp. Bake the pie shell 5 minutes at 425°. Put half the onions in the pie shell. Whisk together the eggs, cottage cheese, and seasonings, pour over the onions, then top with the remaining onions. Bake at 350° until the crust is browned and the cheese mixture set. Serve in wedges as a snack or appetizer.

••••

Chicken McSpeedSnack

Pick up chicken nuggets at a deli, take-out, or fast-food restaurant. To reheat them in the oven, spread in a single layer on a lightly greased baking sheet and bake 5 minutes at 425°. Serve with your own dipping sauces:

•Whisk together ½ c. plain yogurt, ½ c. mayonnaise, 1 t. dill weed, and 1 T. pickle relish.

•Heat a jar of pineapple ice cream topping with a tablespoon of Dijon mustard.

•Heat a jar of orange marmalade with 2 T. soy sauce.

•Whisk together a jar of babyfood blueberry applesauce with ½ c. blueberry preserves and 1 T. of lemon juice over low heat until warm and well blended. Or use babyfood strained plums with plum jelly.

•Mix equal parts of sour cream and salsa.

• Stir together ½ c. honey with 2 T. Dijon mustard and serve hot or cold.

• Stir 1 t. (more to taste) of curry powder into a cup of lemon yogurt.

●●●●

Scurry Curry Chicken Sandwiches

2 cans boneless chunk chicken	½ c. finely diced celery
½ c. raisins	Mayonnaise
½ c. chopped peanuts	16 slices bread
½ t. (or more to taste) curry powder	Butter

Shred the chicken in a bowl and mix in the remaining ingredients with enough mayonnaise to bind. Make 8 sandwiches, using bread or toast.

●●●●

South Pacific Sandwiches

2 c. finely diced cooked chicken
Mayonnaise
¼ t. curry powder
½ t. ground ginger
4 hoagie buns
⅓ c. flaked coconut

Mix the chicken with the curry powder and ginger, and enough mayonnaise to moisten. Cut a generous, full-length trench in each bun and put aside the excess material for another use such as croutons or bread sticks. Pile filling into the buns and sprinkle generously with coconut, pressing it into the filling. Bake on a greased cookie sheet at 400° until heated through and crusty, about 7–10 minutes.

●●●●

Sandwiches Crab Louis

6–8 hotdog buns from a good bakery
Butter
½ c. chili sauce
1 c. mayonnaise
2 hardboiled eggs, diced
3 c. cooked crab or lobster

Slice the buns and open just enough to butter them inside, then toast in a 425° oven just until brown. Mix together the chili sauce and mayo, then fold in the eggs and seafood, and pile into the toasted buns.

●●●●

Tuna Bean Sandwiches

1-lb. can white beans
2 T. olive oil
2 T. lemon juice
Small sweet onion, minced
1 can solid-pack tuna
2 T. fresh minced parsley
Bread or rolls for 4–6 sandwiches

Drain the beans and mash them slightly while adding the olive oil and lemon juice. Add the onion, parsley if you have some (don't substitute dried parsley), and then the tuna, breaking it up as you mix. Use as a sandwich filling.

●●●●

Just for fun, make miniature hotdogs, using finger rolls and cocktail wieners or sausages.

"Crab"wiches

4 English muffins, split and toasted
½ bell pepper, finely diced
2–3 ribs celery, diced
4–5 scallions, finely sliced
1 T. butter
1 lb. imitation crab meat, chopped
2 T. mayonnaise
1 T. lemon juice
1 packet Hollandaise sauce mix

Sauté the vegetables in the butter in a nonstick skillet. Then add the crab and sauté just to heat thoroughly. Stir in the mayonnaise and place some of the mixture on each of the 8 toasted English muffin halves. Make the Hollandaise sauce according to package directions and pour over the crabwiches. Makes 4 servings.

••••

Muffeletta

This is a New Orleans street sandwich, as popular as a "walking" meal as it is in sidewalk cafés. For the RV cook it provides a feast of a sandwich that is made ahead and improves with chilling, so it's ideal to keep in the refrigerator and bring out for a rushed roadside lunch.

16-oz. jar mixed marinated vegetables
2 cloves garlic
6 stuffed olives, sliced
1 T. olive oil
1 unsliced loaf French bread
¼ lb. sliced deli salami
¼ lb. sliced deli provolone cheese

A day or two ahead, open the jar of vegetables, slip in the peeled garlic cloves, return the lid, and put the jar in the refrigerator. To complete the muffeletta, drain the vegetables, discard the garlic, and chop the vegetables coarsely. Cut the loaf in half and dig out some of the bread. Feed it to the birds or save it for another purpose such as making bread crumbs or bread pudding. Brush the cut side of the bread very lightly with olive oil and sprinkle half the vegetables plus some of the sliced olives on the bottom half. Top with overlapping slices of the salami and provolone, then the remaining vegetables and olives. Lid with the top of the loaf. Slice into 4–6 individual servings and wrap each separately in plastic wrap. Chill several hours or overnight.

••••

Sausage-Stuffed Baguette

These can be assembled at home, in advance of a weekend trip, then baked hot and crusty during a quick roadside stop. Don't forget to pick up two 22-inch baguettes (thin French breads) or half a dozen 8-inch French rolls at the deli when you get the other ingredients. Choose the best, leanest sausage in the store.

1 lb. pork sausage
¼ lb. smoked ham, diced
1 c. ricotta cheese
10-oz. pkg. chopped spinach, thawed
1 egg, lightly beaten
¼ c. thinly sliced green onion
French bread or rolls
Olive oil

Fry and drain the sausage. Squeeze all liquid from spinach. Place the spinach in a mixing bowl and mix in remaining ingredients except bread. Slice the bread or rolls in half lengthwise, scoop out some of the filling (save it for bread crumbs to be used later) and brush very lightly with olive oil. Fill with the sausage mixture. Put the halves back together and wrap in foil that has been lightly sprayed with a nonstick coating. Chill at once. To serve, peel back some of foil to expose the bread so it will get crisp and bake at 375° about 30–40 minutes. The filling must be thoroughly heated so the egg and cheese "set." Makes 6 servings.

●●●●

Microwave Reubens

Assemble and wrap these at home a day or two ahead of time. A few minutes in your microwave will heat them up fresh, piquant, and delicious. I'll leave quantities up to you, depending on whether you like sandwiches thick or thin.

Toast big slices of beefsteak rye bread. Butter the bread so it doesn't become soggy. Starting with thinly sliced lean corned beef, add well-drained sauerkraut, Thousand Island dressing, a slice of Swiss cheese, and another slice of corned beef. Top with a second slice of bread, butter side in. Wrap individually in microwave-safe plastic wrap and refrigerate. To serve, heat on High for about 45 seconds each, or until the cheese is melted and the sandwich is heated through.

Variation: Want a low-fat reuben? Make it with thin-sliced deli turkey instead of corned beef.

●●●●

Another use for leftover sandwiches: Arrange them in a buttered baking dish and mix up enough eggs and milk, at a rate of 1 egg to 1 c. milk, to cover completely. Refrigerate several hours or overnight, then bake until it's set, like custard, and serve as a casserole.

Nosebags

Many types of trail mixes are available, or you can invent your own. To achieve a balanced trail "meal," try to maximize cereals with little or no sugar (round oat cereal, bite-size shredded wheat, Chex), minimize fat (nuts, seeds, chocolate bits), and don't overdo the sugar (dried fruit, jellybeans). Measure 1-cup portions into zip-top plastic bags and hit the trail.

Here is a very sweet version. Take it as a "walking" snack or dessert on a long hike after a big meal.

½ c. toasted pecan or walnut halves
½ c. sunflower seeds
2 c. pitted prunes, dried apricots, raisins, cut up
½ c. coarsely shredded coconut
½ c. banana chips

Makes 4 nosebags, 1 cup each.

●●●●

Creamy Clam Spread

6-oz. can minced clams
10¾-oz. can condensed cream of chicken soup
8-oz. pkg. cream cheese
¼ c. ketchup
Small sweet onion, finely diced

Drain the clams and let cream cheese come to room temperature. Mash everything together with a fork or with the electric mixer until it's smooth. Spread on crackers for snacks or make sandwiches by spreading generously on buttered bread and topping with a lettuce leaf.

●●●●

Poor Folks' Pâté

This is a healthful alternative to junk-food snacking. It's a breeze to make at home in your food processor. Then press it into a lidded container and keep cold. Serve it with crackers.

Med. onion, chopped	2 T. sherry
1 T. virgin olive oil	⅛ t. ground nutmeg
1-lb. can green beans, drained	Freshly ground pepper
2 hard-cooked eggs, quartered	1–2 T. mayonnaise
¼ c. toasted sunflower seeds	

Sauté the onion in the oil, then process with the beans, eggs, and sunflower seeds. Mix in sherry, nutmeg, and pepper and add just enough mayo to bind it. The mixture should be stiff. Press it into a lightly greased crock or mold. It can be served from the crock but makes an impressive presentation if you unmold it and serve it in slices.

●●●●

Bacon Wraps

Cut a pound of bacon in half and fasten each piece around a filling. Fasten with a toothpick and bake at 375° for about 15 minutes or until the bacon is done. Drain on paper towel, then transfer to a serving plate.

For fillings, try:

Water chestnuts
Watermelon-rind pickles
Artichoke-heart halves
Whole oysters
Halved chicken livers
Chunks of fresh pineapple
Wedges of fresh apple
Parboiled broccoli or cauliflower florets
Giant stuffed olives

●●●●

Shortcut Soft Pretzels

If you have frozen bread dough on hand, bring it out on a rainy day and let the children work the dough and tie the knots. If you have coarse salt on hand, so much the better. Butter-flavored popcorn salt is a good choice too, or just use regular salt.

1 loaf frozen bread dough
1 egg
1 T. water

Divide the loaf into 16 pieces. Roll each piece between your hands to form a long rope, then tie into knot-like shapes. If this is a family project, you might even turn it into a knot-tying contest. Place on greased baking sheets and let rise until light. Beat the egg and water together and brush on the pretzels. Sprinkle with salt. Bake at 375° for 10–15 minutes or until evenly browned. Real pretzels are boiled before baking, so these will have a lighter and more bread-like texture, but slather them with yellow mustard and nobody will care.

●●●●

Fast Lane

•Melt 3 T. butter, add 3 cloves garlic, minced, and 1½ t. Tabasco. Cook 1 minute. Toss with 3 c. pecan halves and spread on a baking sheet. Bake for 1 hour at 250°, stirring occasionally. Cool.

•Make a fiery, low-fat dip by combining 1 c. yogurt, 2 c. cottage cheese, ½ c. chopped red onion, 2½ t. ground cumin, and 45 drops (¾ t.) Tabasco in a blender. Blend smooth, chill, and serve with raw vegetables.

•Rediscover apple butter as a satiny sandwich spread. It glides on more evenly than most jellies, and it combines deliciously with peanut butter, sliced bananas, crumbled bacon, or spreadable cream cheese.

•Add zest to a sliced turkey sandwich by spreading it with

mayo, then cranberry-orange relish.

•Add milk to biscuit dough to make a thick batter. Dip slices of banana, apple, or other firm, fresh fruit, and deep-fry until crusty brown. Serve as a snack with syrup or powdered sugar.

•Shave calories by substituting plain, nonfat yogurt for sour cream in dips.

•To make a quick dip for raw vegetables, stir 1 t. (or more to taste) curry powder into a carton of lemon yogurt.

•Instead of using tortilla chips, use nacho sauce with frozen French fries, browned in the oven, to make a hot, filling snack.

•To turn toasted cheese sandwiches into a knife and fork meal, heat a can of broccoli cheese soup with ¼ c. milk in the microwave on High for 3–5 minutes. Stir and spoon over hot and crusty sandwiches.

•Use finely diced fennel root as part of the celery measurement in chicken salad sandwich filling.

8

Menu Makers: Meat and Poultry

For more recipes utilizing meat, see chapters on One-Dish Meals, Soups, Slow Cookery and Rainy-Day Fare, and Anytime Foods.

Peanut Sauce Lamb Satay

This recipe comes from the American Lamb Council. If you're tired of the same old grilled meats, try this exciting blend of flavors. Do the first steps at home and keep the meat, marinating in a plastic bag, in your RV refrigerator to use the first day out. A derivative of an Indonesian recipe that calls for hot pepper, this one is milder. If you like, add your favorite hot pepper to the peanut sauce.

1¼ lb. boneless lamb leg, well trimmed
½ c. lime juice
20-oz. can pineapple chunks in juice
5 T. creamy peanut butter

Ask the butcher to cut the lamb into thin strips about 1 inch wide and 3 inches long, or freeze it partially to make it easier to cut it yourself. Put the meat and the lime juice in a plastic bag and refrigerate several hours or overnight. Drain the meat and pat dry, then thread on skewers. If you're using bamboo skewers, soak them in water for an hour first. Broil over well-started coals 6–7 minutes, turning once.

Sauce: Put the peanut butter in a small saucepan and, over low heat, gradually stir in the juice from the pineapple. Cook and stir until hot and smooth. Garnish the meat with the pineapple chunks and give each person a small cup of the peanut sauce for dipping. Serves 4.

Complete the menu with fruited rice, a tart salad, soft bread sticks, and plain butter cookies with jasmine tea.

●●●●

Quick Curried Pork

The secret to developing the flavor of curry powder is to sauté it in the oil before liquids are added.

1 lb. lean, boneless pork	2 T. curry powder
2 T. oil	2 T. cornstarch
1 rib celery	1 chicken bouillon cube
½ sweet red pepper	1½ c. water
½ sweet green pepper	10-oz. pkg. frozen peas
2–3 scallions	

Slice the pork in thin rings. Dice the vegetables. In a roomy skillet brown the pork in the hot oil. Continue stir-frying while adding the vegetables, then the curry powder. When the pork is no longer pink and the vegetables are crisp-tender, add a mixture of the water and cornstarch. Stir in the chicken bouillon and cook, stirring, over medium heat until the sauce is thick and clear. Stir in the peas until they are heated through. Serves 4.

Complete the meal with white rice, a jellied apple salad, cinnamon apple tea, and coconut custard pie.

●●●●

Pork Chop Bake

6 lean pork chops
6 hard, tart baking apples
Raisins
Walnuts
Maple syrup
2-lb. can sauerkraut

Brown the pork chops well on both sides in a nonstick skillet. Rinse and drain the sauerkraut and spread it in a large, shallow baking pan or oven-to-table baking dish. Core the apples and fill with a mixture of raisins and chopped nuts. Arrange the pork chops and apples atop the sauerkraut, drizzle the apples with syrup, and bake at 350° for about 45 minutes or until apples are done.

●●●●

Pork Chop Skillet

For each serving:
1 lean, meaty, boneless pork chop
1 canned pineapple ring
1 ring sliced from a green pepper
1 dried apricot half
1 pitted dried prune
Wine for deglazing pan

In a roomy skillet brown pork chops on both sides. Reduce heat. Top each chop with a pineapple ring and top that with a green pepper ring. In the center of each ring place a prune stuffed with an apricot. Add the juice from the canned pineapple, cover, and braise over low heat about 20 minutes or until the chops are tender and done through. Arrange on plates, reduce any remaining cooking liquid, and deglaze the pan with sherry or Marsala wine, then drizzle over chops. Serve with stovetop cornbread dressing, steamed broccoli, and fresh fruit for dessert.

Variation: Try ½-inch-thick rings cut from seeded acorn squash instead of the pineapple and green pepper. Use a little water for braising.

••••

Pit Stop Beef Wellington

OK, so a cordon bleu chef would blanch at this shortcut version, but try it on for size. It has long been one of my show-off, company-best RV presentations. Guests, especially non-RVers who think we campers live on hardtack and canned beans, gasp when this is carved. The beef should be pink inside, so don't waste this on people who are grossed out by meat that is rare to medium rare.

About 3 lbs. beef tenderloin
1 pkg. puff pastry
8-oz. can liver pâté
1 egg

Sprinkle the beef with salt and pepper and roast 20–30 minutes at 425°. Inside should be red, outside brown. Thaw the puff pastry and roll it thin on a floured cloth or paper towel. When the roast is cool enough, frost the top with the pâté. Cover with the pastry, sealing seams with a finger wet with water and place, seam side down (pâté side up), on a clean, greased baking pan. Beat the egg with a little water and brush it on the pastry. Bake 30–35 minutes or until the pastry is brown and crusty, at 400°. Let stand 15 minutes, then cut into servings 1–2 inches thick.

••••

Fruited Chicken

2 lbs. skinned chicken thighs
2 T. olive oil
1 can condensed cream of
   chicken soup
¾ c. orange juice
Lg. onion, diced
2 cloves garlic, minced

2 T. slivered almonds
2 T. raisins
¼ t. apple pie spice
¼ t. turmeric
Fresh orange sections
Hot rice

In a large skillet brown chicken in the oil and pour off fat. Cover with all the remaining ingredients except the oranges and simmer, covered, over low-medium flame for 45 minutes or until chicken is tender. Place chicken on serving plates atop a bed of rice. Stir sauce and pour over chicken. Garnish with orange sections. This goes well with tiny green peas, carrot-cabbage slaw, a fruity quick bread such as cranberry loaf, and a light, lemony dessert.

••••

Chicken Rice Pot Pie

The next time you have leftover rice and leftover chicken at home, bag and freeze them to make this on your next RV trip. If you like, the entire pie can be put together at home the night before. Just keep it well refrigerated until you bake it.

Pastry for 2-crust, 9-inch pie
Med. onion, diced
2 cloves garlic, minced
2 stalks celery, diced
2 T. butter
1 can condensed cream
   of chicken soup

⅓ c. milk
1½ c. diced, cooked chicken
   (or two cans boneless chicken)
1 T. lemon juice
1½ c. cooked rice
4 hardboiled eggs

Line a pie pan with pastry. Sauté the onion, celery, and garlic in butter until softened, then mix in the soup, milk, chicken, and lemon juice. Alternate layers of rice, sliced eggs, and the chicken mixture in the pastry, then add the top crust, seal, trim edges, and flute. Bake at 375° until brown. Time will vary. Taken from the refrigerator, the pie will take as long as one hour. If it is freshly made with hot filling, it will brown in as little as 35–45 minutes. Serves 6–8.

Complete the meal with a big platter of crunchy and colorful relishes, whole-cranberry sauce, and a "walking" dessert such as Pocket Pretzels or crisp apples to enjoy on a postprandial hike.

●●●●

Microwave Turkey Divan

10-oz. pkg. frozen broccoli spears
8 slices deli breast of turkey
10½-oz. can cream of chicken soup
Pinch nutmeg
4 T. dry white wine
6-oz. pkg. grated cheese

Lay out two slices of turkey, overlapping, and place a stalk or two of broccoli on them. Roll up and place on a microwave platter. Repeat with remaining turkey and broccoli. Combine soup, wine, nutmeg, and cheese in a quart-size microwave cooking container and cook on High for 2 minutes. Pour over turkey rolls and cover with plastic cooking wrap vented at one corner. Cook on High 8–10 minutes, rotating once. Let stand a few minutes before serving.

Complete the meal with microwave-baked potatoes, a green salad, monkey bread, and a dessert of instant vanilla pudding drowning in frozen strawberries thawed to slushiness.

●●●●

Cut leftover meatloaf or salmon loaf into chunks and wrap each serving in thawed puff pastry dough, rolled as thin as possible. Bake at 425° until brown and serve with a simple sauce made by stirring fresh or dried dill into a mixture of half mayo and half yogurt.

Janet's Chicken and Dumplings

I've made it with home-canned chicken thighs, commercially canned whole chicken, and fresh chicken parts. This is a comfort food classic I serve at least once a week when we're on the go. By cooking carrot and celery chunks with it, I make a complete meal in one pot, and the vegetables make for a richer gravy too. If you can throw in a handful of thawed peas or chopped parsley just before serving, the dish will be even more colorful.

4 servings chicken
4 carrots, in chunks
2 cloves garlic
3 ribs celery, sliced
2 c. biscuit mix

If you're using canned chicken, bone it and place it in a roomy pot with the garlic. If the chicken is fresh, brown it and the garlic in a little olive oil. Now add a couple of inches of water and the carrots and celery, cover, and simmer while stirring the dumplings. Simply add water or milk to biscuit mix to make a stiff dough and drop it by teaspoons atop the boiling liquid. Keep the liquid boiling 10 minutes, uncovered (make sure it doesn't boil dry), then cover the pot, lower the flame, and cook 10 minutes more. Stir in the peas or parsley and serve at once. Dumplings get soggy if they are kept waiting.

●●●●

Try using graham cracker crumbs instead of saltine crumbs in ham loaf.

To create a pattern in a meatloaf, add strips of cooked whole carrot and green beans when pressing the mixture into the pan. Or put half the meat in the pan, then add a line of hardboiled eggs before topping with the rest of the meat mixture. Bake and slice.

Stovetop Meatloaf and Baked Potatoes

To save water, scrub the potatoes at home and wrap them in clean paper towels. To save clean-up, mix the meatloaf in a disposable bag. When you want a quick meatloaf without having to heat the oven, try this crusty, fragrant, skillet loaf and browned potatoes.

1 lb. lean ground beef
2 T. dried onion flakes
1 t. salt, dash pepper
⅓ c. raw oatmeal
1 egg
2 lg. baking potatoes
1 can cream of mushroom soup (optional) for gravy

Smoosh meatloaf makings together in a plastic freezer bag (regular bags are thin and may tear) until well mixed. Turn out into a cold, lightly greased, heavy skillet (preferably cast aluminum) for which you have a heavy, tight-fitting lid. Shape into a mound in the center of the skillet, leaving room around the edges for potatoes. Cut each potato in half and place, cut side down, in the skillet. Cover and bake over a medium-low flame 45–60 minutes. Cut the meatloaf into 4 wedges and serve with the baked potatoes, gravy (made by stirring a can of condensed cream of mushroom soup into the pan drippings), crusty rolls, and a leafy salad glistening with cheesy vinaigrette dressing.

●●●●

Boneless Bonanza Roast

If you have to serve a crowd out of your small oven, get a boneless roast. Roast according to cookbook directions for lamb, pork, or rolled breast of turkey and smother it with this sauce.

1 sweet red pepper	1 T. cornstarch
1 green bell pepper	1 T. vinegar
Med. onion	2 t. sugar
8-oz. can Mandarin oranges	Splash Worcestershire sauce
8-oz. can corn	2 T. sherry

Dice the vegetables. Drain the corn and oranges and gradually mix the cornstarch into all of the liquids in a saucepan or microwave container. Add remaining ingredients and cook, stirring frequently, until thick and clear. Pour over roast for last 45 minutes of baking time.

Variation: Substitute crushed pineapple for the corn.

••••

Ginger Chicken

4 slices bacon, diced	4 boneless chicken breasts
1 t. curry powder	2 t. ginger
Lg. onion, diced	4 firm bananas
2 cloves garlic, minced	2 hardboiled eggs
1 c. water	⅓ c. raisins
1 chicken bouillon cube	

Fry the bacon in a large skillet until it's crisp, then pour off all but about 2 tablespoons of the fat. Add the curry powder, onion, and garlic and sauté until they are limp, then add the water and bouillon cube. Stir to dissolve.

Lay out chicken flat, sprinkle with ginger, and form into bundles. Place chicken bundles atop the hot sauce in the skillet, then ladle more sauce over them. Cover and simmer over low flame 10 minutes, then baste again and add the bananas, cut into chunks, the chopped eggs, and the raisins. Cover and cook 10 minutes more or until chicken is tender. Arrange a bed of rice on each plate, top with the chicken, stir sauce, and ladle it over the chicken and rice.

●●●●

Springtime Ham Rolls

Because you buy the meat in the deli, it is fully cooked and sliced to order. This recipe serves two, and it's easy to multiply it to feed any number of happy campers. I can have it on the table 20 minutes after we've hooked up at the campground.

8–10 stalks fresh asparagus
6 oz. deli baked, sliced ham
2 T. oil
1 clove garlic, minced
2 T. seasoned bread crumbs
2 T. grated cheddar

Wash and trim the asparagus and sauté the whole stalks in hot oil with the garlic until the asparagus is just crisp-tender. While it's cooking, lay out the ham in overlapping slices to form two rectangles. Arrange the asparagus in bundles on the ham. Frazzle the bread crumbs in the skillet in the remaining oil and bits of garlic, and sprinkle over the asparagus. Top each with a tuft of cheese. Roll up and place, seam side down, on a baking pan. Bake 10 minutes at 350°. Add big slabs of hot cornbread glistening with honey butter and mugs of hot cranberry tea to make the meal. Another good way to serve these rolls is in hero sandwich buns that have been buttered and toasted.

●●●●

Brown large batches of a mixture of ground meat, diced green and red peppers, onion and garlic. Drain off excess fat. Freeze mixture in 2-cup (1-pound) batches. It will be ready each time you make a recipe that starts with browned ground meat, onions, and peppers.

Steak Port Antonio

This recipe was developed by the people who make Tabasco sauce. Let's name names. There is no substitute for the original Tabasco sauce. I make this sauce in a small, nonstick skillet.

¼ c. rum
1 T. chopped shallots
¼ lb. butter
2 t. lime juice
½ t. Tabasco pepper sauce
1 T. chopped parsley
4 servings your favorite steak

Combine rum and shallots, bring to a boil, and simmer 2 minutes. Stir in remaining ingredients. Broil or grill steaks, brushing with rum butter, until done to your satisfaction.

●●●●

The Magic of Marinade

The outdoor grill is the RV cook's second stove, and many families cook every dinner outdoors. To become an expert barbecue chef is not easy; to succeed in camping, where you're using different grills each time according to what the campsite provides, is difficult indeed. By using marinades you can even the odds by getting a more reliable flavor and tenderness.

An entire cookbook can be filled with recipes for marinades, but the truth is that they boil down to certain basics according to their country of origin. Here, from the National Pork Producers Council, is a summary of the flavors that go into each type of marinade. Because the flavors steal so subtly into the meat, and their intensity depends as much on the length of the marinating as on the strength of the spices, amounts can be fairly flexible—using, of course, your own good judgment about proportions. In each case the chief ingredient is listed first. Use enough to coat the meat well. Other ingredients are added in smaller amounts. Marinating is best done in a well-sealed plastic bag that can be turned and tumbled repeatedly for even distribution of flavors.

- Caribbean: lime juice, oregano, thyme, allspice
- Indian: yogurt, crushed ginger and garlic, ground coriander, cumin, turmeric, red pepper
- Mediterranean: wine or vinegar, olive oil, garlic, oregano, rosemary
- Oriental: soy sauce, garlic, ginger, sesame oil
- Southwestern: cider vinegar, onion, ground chili, cumin, oregano
- Scandinavian: oil, lemon, dill or cardamom

Basic marinade rules:

- Meat should always be refrigerated while marinating.
- Once raw meat has been in a marinade, the marinade should never be used except as a baste as the meat cooks. If it is to be served as a sauce with the meat, cook it thoroughly.
- Don't marinate meat in a metal container.
- Marinades that contain highly sugared ingredients such as honey or ketchup tend to carbonize sooner. Meats and poultry that require long, thorough cooking are best basted with sweet sauces toward the end of their cooking time.

MINIMUM MARINATING TIMES

Strips, thin chops	30 minutes–2 hours
Cubes for kabob	1–24 hours
Thick chops	2–24 hours
Boneless roasts, 1–5 lbs.	12–24 hours
Boneless roasts, 5 lbs.+	24–72 hours
Bone-in roasts, 4–12 lbs.	12–14 hours
Dry-rub ribs	12–24 hours

> To make a boneless roast more interesting, stab randomly
> with an ice pick and force in peeled garlic cloves, raisins,
> and pistachios to various depths. They'll add flavor and,
> when the roast is sliced, they will form an interesting
> mosaic pattern.

Newer Skewers

Kabobs are the quickest and most versatile way to barbecue. Here are some ideas to string you along:

- Alternate chunks of light and dark sausages.
- Make surf-and-turfabobs by threading parboiled chunks of boneless, skinless chicken breast with whole shrimp or chunks of lobster. Parboiled chicken cooks faster, so you don't overcook the delicate seafood.
- Weave strips of boneless chicken breast with small pieces of a highly spiced sausage. The bland chicken tames the sausage; the fatty sausage bastes the dry chicken.

●●●●

Pork Chops Adobo

This is a simple recipe because it has only a few ingredients, but its flavors are rich and complex. The secret is the marinade, which can easily be started at home. Unlike most other recipes for marinated meats, this one calls for skillet cooking, so it's an ideal indoor barbecue. Flavor intensity increases with time. Give it at least 4 hours, and up to 24.

4–8 boneless pork loin chops, about 4 oz. each	2 cloves garlic, crushed
12-oz. jar jalapeño peppers, undrained	2 t. ground cumin
4 t. oregano	4 T. cider vinegar
	1 t. oil

Combine everything but the chops and oil in the blender to make a purée and marinate the chops in it. Heat the oil in a nonstick skillet and pan broil the chops 5 minutes on each side. Serve with cold broccoli vinaigrette, Mexicorn from a can, hot cornbread with honey butter, and a fresh fruit salad splashed with apple brandy for dessert.

●●●●

Panfastic Beef Stroganoff

The secret to the quick, tender cooking of this stovetop Stroganoff is to slice the beef thinly, slanting across the grain. This is easier if the meat is partially frozen first. I sometimes do this step at home and carry the sliced beef sealed in a plastic bag, in the coldest spot in the refrigerator.

1½ lb. lean top round or London broil	8-oz. can mushrooms
1 t. oil	½ c. liquid (water plus juice from mushrooms)
1 T. instant-blend flour (available in the flour section from both Pillsbury and Gold Medal)	Med. onion, finely diced
	1 T. Dijon mustard
1 t. salt	½ c. sour cream
Dash pepper	Fresh parsley

Stir-fry the steak slices in the oil in a hot, nonstick skillet until browned. Drain the mushrooms and stir the flour into the cold liquid, then add the liquid, mushrooms, and salt and pepper to the pan. Cook over medium flame, stirring, until the mixture thickens. Stir the mustard into the sour cream and add it just until it's heated. Don't let it boil.

This makes 6 helpings to serve over instant mashed potatoes or rice. Sprinkle it with chopped parsley and complete the plate with boil-in-the-bag buttered peas and carrots and a slab of chilled tomato aspic. Pass out candy bar–size peppermint patties, grab the dog's leash, and go on a brisk walk while you savor dessert.

••••

Pantabulous Turkeyburgers

The ginger gives these burgers an exotic Oriental tang. Pass the soy sauce at the table to bring out the taste even more.

1 lb. lean ground turkey	Few bits candied ginger,
Small onion, minced	minced
Celery stalk, minced	⅓ c. raw oatmeal
Green pepper, minced	Oil for frying
1 t. salt (omit if you're	
serving soy sauce)	

Knead all ingredients together in a heavy-duty plastic bag. Rinse your hands in cold water and form the meat into 4 patties. Fry in a little hot oil in a nonstick skillet until brown, then turn, cover, and cook over a medium flame until well browned on the other side. Set the patties aside and cover them to stay warm while you stir-fry a medley of your favorite cut-up vegetables in the same pan just until they're crisp-tender. Complete the meal with your favorite rice.

••••

Skillet Spare Ribs

4 servings lean baby spareribs,	Cooking oil
(about 2½ lbs.) cut into	1 c. beef broth
pieces containing 2–3 ribs each	8 dried apricots
1 c. white wine or grape juice	3 T. cornstarch
1 jar strained babyfood apricots	Salt, pepper

Marinate the ribs overnight in a mixture of the wine and apricots in a plastic bag that can be turned from time to time. Drain the ribs, reserving the marinade, and brown them on both sides in hot oil in a large skillet. Add the reserved marinade, the beef broth, and the fruit. Cover and simmer until the ribs are tender, about an hour. Mix cold water with the cornstarch to make a paste, then remove the ribs and fruit from the pan and pile them onto serving plates. Quickly stir the paste into the pan juices over a high flame until the sauce is thickened and clear, adding more water or bouillon if necessary. Salt and pepper to taste. Spoon the sauce over the ribs and fruit and serve with steamed white rice (mix in a cup of thawed green peas for the last minute of cooking), a salad, and vanilla ice cream sauced with hot apple pie filling.

●●●●

Schinken Schnitzel

This is a quick way to make an old favorite without having to pound cutlets to make them thin enough. You start with fully cooked boiled ham, cut to order at the deli.

1 lb. boiled ham
2 eggs
2 T. water
About 1 c. bread crumbs
1 t. thyme
1 T. grated Parmesan cheese
Hot oil for frying

Have the ham sliced 8 slices to the pound. Cut each in half. Beat together the eggs and water. Dip ham slices into the eggs, then into the bread crumbs mixed with the thyme and cheese. Fry in hot oil until brown and crispy. This makes 16 slices; serve 2–4 per person.

●●●●

CHAPTER NINE

Seafood: Fishing for Compliments

Fishing and RV travel have been best buddies since the dawn of wheeled camping. In assembling these recipes I have kept in mind that some people fish to eat, some fish to release, some buy their fish in markets, and others buy their fish in cans.

Even if you're an ardent and successful fisherman, I recommend that you keep some canned seafood on hand for those times when you don't land as many fish as you'd planned. The best chowders and bouillabaisses are those made with a variety of flavors. By augmenting a small catch with canned shrimp, crab, oysters, mussels, or tuna, you can create a combination far more exotic and exciting than the plain fish meal you had planned to serve.

If you're grilling a large, whole fish, here's how to get a grip on it. Tear off two sheets of foil about 5 inches long, and fold lengthwise four times to make long, strong strips about 1 inch wide. Put one around each end of the fish, fore and aft, and twist the ends to make tabs. Lay the fish on a greased grill, using the tabs to turn it over and roll it onto a serving platter.

Fruity Fish Salad

Use tidbits of leftover fish or poach a pound of boneless fish to make this zesty salad. For a more economical dish use 3 cups of leftover brown or white rice instead of the mix, then add your own herbs and spices to taste.

2 c. cold, cooked fish pieces
Pkg. rice and wild rice mix, prepared
1 c. diced celery
1 c. diced red apple
1 c. halved seedless grapes
1 c. poppy seed or buttermilk dressing
Lettuce cups
Raisins, slivered almonds

Toss rice, fish, fruit, and vegetables lightly with the dressing. Spoon into 4 lettuce cups and sprinkle with raisins and slivered almonds. Add rolls or crackers, and it's a complete meal.

••••

Oyster Pudding

Cornbread and oysters are natural friends. Make a double batch of cornbread at breakfast time and save half for this one-dish dinner. Cook the extra bacon at breakfast time too.

About 2 c. cornbread, crumbled
1 lb. oysters, drained
Juice of ½ lemon
8-oz. can mushroom stems
and pieces, drained
½ c. each chopped sweet onion,
green pepper, celery

Clove garlic, minced
2 T. butter
4 thick slices bacon, cooked and
diced
2 eggs
¾ c. milk

If the oysters are large, cut them into bite-size pieces and arrange in a buttered pan, casserole, or deep pie dish. Sprinkle with the lemon juice, mushrooms, and bacon. Sauté the vegetables in butter until they're crisp-tender, then sprinkle them over the oyster mixture. Beat eggs and milk and stir in the cornbread to make a thick batter. Pour it over the oyster mixture and bake until set, about 35 minutes, at 350°. Serves 4–6.

●●●●

Lobster (or Crab) Sandwiches

One of my friends once gave me a recipe that called for "as many pecans as you can afford." That's the case with these sandwiches, in which a little lobster or crab goes a long, flavorful way. They're best made with big, rich, buttery buns from a good bakery.

16-oz. pkg. shredded cabbage
   for cole slaw
1 T. sugar
¾ c. mayonnaise

Med. sweet onion, diced
8–16 oz., depending on the
   budget, cooked lobster or crab
Hotdog buns

Sprinkle the cabbage with the sugar. Shred or finely chop the crab or lobster. Toss everything together and pile into hotdog buns. This is best if it's assembled just before serving.

●●●●

Individual Pizzas

This is another way to stretch a small catch, or to use bits of leftover cooked fish.

Flour tortillas, 1–2 per
   person
Cooking oil
Can or jar pizza sauce

Bermuda onion
Poached fish, cooled
1 avocado
Monterey Jack cheese

Fry each tortilla in a little oil until browned and puffy, and drizzle lightly with pizza sauce. Strew with onion slices, chunks of fish, thinly sliced avocado, then the cheese. Bake in a 450° oven just long enough to heat through and melt the cheese. Although this takes some quick juggling in a small oven, baking time is fairly short so it works out if you set up an assembly line.

●●●●

Fish in Foil

Have you noticed how important mustard has become in today's recipes? There are many types and flavors on the market. This is a good recipe for use with a classic Dijon mustard or, if you're more daring, one of the exotic mustards such as raspberry, green peppercorn, or hazelnut.

4 fillets fresh fish	1 T. fancy mustard
4 slices sweet onion	Lemon juice
4 sprigs parsley	Thyme
⅓ c. mayonnaise	

Set out 4 squares of foil and place a slice of onion on each. Sprinkle with chopped parsley, then add a piece of fish. Whisk the mustard, lemon juice, and mayo together and pour over the fish. Sprinkle lightly with thyme. Double fold the fish, and bake atop a well-started grill about 10 minutes on each side, then test. Cook until the fish flakes easily and is firm throughout. While you're at it, grill corn on the cob or zucchini kabobs. Complete the meal with canned potato salad, muffins from the bakery, and popcorn balls for a dessert to munch on while taking a brisk walk.

●●●●

It's easy to can surplus fish if you have jars and a pressure cooker. Ask your county home economist for directions, depending on the kinds of fish you angle for. In some parts of the country public canneries also cater to fishermen.

Cioppino

There are as many recipes for this classic Mediterranean fish stew as there are Mediterranean cooks. If you carry canned clams, you'll be able to rustle up cioppino by catching or buying a good, firm, meaty fish. Buy canned clams with shells, and your cioppino will look authentic too.

⅓ c. olive oil	1 c. dry red wine
Lg. onion, diced	1 T. Italian seasoning
Bell pepper, diced	2 to 2½ lbs. fish fillets
1 t. salt	10 ounces canned clams
2, 1-lb. cans tomatoes	or a dozen fresh clams
8-oz. can tomato sauce	Fresh parsley

Use your largest skillet or a roomy pot. Sauté the onion and pepper in the olive oil, then add the garlic, tomatoes, tomato sauce, wine, and herbs. Bring to a boil, reduce heat, and simmer half an hour. Add the fish in bite-size chunks, bring to a boil, arrange clams on top, and simmer just until the fish is firm and clams open. Ladle into soup plates, arranging a clam or two on each serving, and sprinkle with chopped fresh parsley. Center a crusty loaf of French or Italian bread on the table so each person can tear off pieces as desired to soak up the flavorful juices.

●●●●

Make a batter for deep-fried fish by adding beer, ginger ale, lemon-lime soda, white wine diluted with water, or cola to pancake mix until it's like thick cream. Dip in chunks of fish and drop into sizzling fat.

Smoked Fish Casserole

Many RV travelers enjoy smoking their own fish. Or buy it as you go, experimenting with wonderful varieties—from smoked salmon in the Pacific Northwest to smoked kingfish and mullet in Florida. Then make this tangy, unusual, lowfat casserole.

1 lb. smoked fish
8-oz. package noodles
1-lb. container creamy cottage cheese
Clove garlic, minced
1 c. unflavored yogurt
Small bunch scallions, sliced
Grated Romano or Parmesan cheese

Skin, bone, and shred the fish. Set aside. Cook and drain noodles. Mix everything except the grated cheese and put in a buttered casserole. Sprinkle lightly with grated cheese and bake in a 350° oven for about 25 minutes or until thoroughly heated. Serve with rye rolls, carrot and celery sticks, and fresh fruit cocktail for dessert.

●●●●

It's messy to dip fish in egg, then bread crumbs. Instead, pat fish dry with paper towels and spread fillets with mayonnaise, then dip in seasoned crumbs or cornmeal you have spread on a paper plate.

Seafood Stew

Corn adds a sweetness to the seafood; crisp nuggets of salt pork add a traditional touch. If you make it from canned fish, get as much variety as possible: tuna, crab, shrimp, salmon. Or use fresh fish. It's a quick, hearty warmer on a cold night. Cans called for are 14–16 ounces each; substitute canned peas if you can't manage frozen.

8 oz. salt pork, cut into dice-size cubes
3 lg. onions, diced
1 lb. boneless seafood, in chunks
1 can cream-style corn
2 cans potatoes
2 cans tomatoes
10-oz. pkg. frozen peas, thawed
Salt, pepper, butter, thyme

In a big, heavy kettle, fry out the salt pork until it's crisp, remove to paper towel, and sizzle the onions in the fat until they're limp. Discard excess fat. Put the seafood, corn, rinsed and drained potatoes, and the tomatoes with their juice into the pot and simmer gently about 30 minutes, stirring occasionally. Stir in the peas, salt, and pepper just before serving. In each soup bowl place a pat of butter and sprinkle it with thyme, then ladle in the soup. Sprinkle with pork tidbits. Serves 4–6.

Serve with pilot crackers, a side dish of deli cole slaw, and saucer-size molasses cookies for dessert.

●●●●

Seafood Pasta Primavera

The beauty of this recipe is that you can prepare the vegetables at home, ready to stir-fry the moment your ship comes in. The entire brightly fresh meal throws together in one big skillet or wok. The pasta, too, can be cooked at home. Rinse it in cold water and drain it well, tossing it with a tablespoon of olive oil to keep it from sticking. Then pile it lightly into a container and keep cold until needed.

1 lb. linguine, cooked al dente
1 T. peanut oil
Lg. onion, diced
3 cloves garlic, minced
1 lb. fresh asparagus, cut into
    ½-inch slices
4 c. fresh vegetables, cut up
    (mushrooms, broccoli and

cauliflower florets, zucchini,
    bok choy)
2 T. mixed Italian herbs
2 lbs. fresh, boneless seafood
    in bite-size bits
1 c. frozen peas, thawed
Freshly grated Parmesan

Sizzle the onion and garlic in hot oil in a large wok or skillet. Keeping heat high, stir-fry in the other vegetables, herbs, and fish. Cook just until the vegetables are crisp-tender and any fresh fish is cooked through. Lightly toss in pasta and peas and stir-fry until everything is heated through. Remove from heat. Sprinkle with cheese, toss again, and serve. Just add a green salad and kaiser rolls slathered with butter, and you've made a banquet for 6–8.

●●●●

Fish Paprika

This is another soupy stew that needs only a crusty loaf to complete the meal. It originated in Hungary, where less desirable fish are placed in a layer at the bottom of the kettle so their juices can enhance the dish. They are not eaten. The pot is shaken, never stirred. Make it on the stove or over the fire.

4 lbs. fish fillets
3 lg. onions (2 lbs.)
Water

1 T. sweet paprika
Salt to taste
Yogurt or sour cream

Starting with fish, layer sliced onions and fish in a large kettle and cover with water. Bring to boiling, add paprika and salt, cover, and simmer over low flame about 40 minutes, shaking the pot occasionally. Using a draining spoon skim off servings of fish and onion and place in serving bowls. Strain the broth into a pitcher and pour over the fish. Top each with a dollop of yogurt or sour cream.

••••

Make-ahead Spaghetti in Clam Sauce

Assemble this casserole at home, and all you have to do is bake it until it's bubbly and fragrant.

1 lb. thin spaghetti	2 t. mixed Italian herbs
3 cans clams	Fresh, chopped parsley
¾ c. extra virgin olive oil	⅓ c. freshly grated
8 cloves garlic	Parmesan cheese
Bottled clam juice	

Cook the spaghetti until it's barely tender and arrange it in a buttered casserole. Sprinkle with chopped clams, reserving clam juice. In the same pot, heat the olive oil and cook the coarsely chopped garlic until it's lightly browned. Add bottled juice to the clam juice to make 3 cups, add it to the garlic mixture, stir in the parsley, and pour over the spaghetti. Bake it now or cover and refrigerate it to serve within the next day or two.

To bake: Cover with grated cheese and bake, uncovered, at 350° until it's heated through—about 15 minutes for a hot casserole, 30–35 if it has been refrigerated. Serves 4.

Complete the menu with baguettes of bread, a leafy salad, and Coffee Galliano.

••••

Leftover cooked fillets of fish? Roll out a tube of crescent-roll dough, sealing perforations, and cut into four portions. Fold around four chunks of seasoned, cooked fish, moistening the edges to make a sealed package. Bake at 350° for 25 minutes or until brown and puffy.

Stuffed Eggplant Seaside

2 med. eggplants
1 T. butter
1 T. olive oil
Med. onion, diced
2–3 ribs celery, diced

2 cloves garlic, minced
1 lb. shrimp, peeled and deveined
½ c. Italian bread crumbs
2 T. butter, melted

Cut the eggplants in half lengthwise and scoop them out (a grapefruit spoon makes a good digger) leaving a wall about ⅛ inch thick. Melt the butter and olive oil together in a skillet and sauté the onion, celery, garlic, and diced eggplant until just tender, then stir in the shrimp and cook another few minutes until the shrimp turns firm and pink. Stir in ⅛ cup of the crumbs and pile the mixture into the eggplant "boats." Top with the remaining crumbs and drizzle with the remaining butter. Bake on a cookie sheet 25 minutes at 350°. Garnish with lemon wedges and serve with soft rolls and a side salad of sliced oranges and Bermuda onion rings drizzled with French dressing.

Note: After the eggplant shells are filled with the hot mixture, you can wrap them individually and refrigerate to bake the next day. Increase baking time to about 45 minutes to assure that the "boats" are steamy throughout.

●●●●

Clamdigger Pie

6-oz. can chopped clams
6-oz. can chunk salmon
2 eggs
Small can (⅔ c.) evaporated milk
10-oz. pkg. frozen, chopped
    spinach

¼ t. nutmeg
2 c. mashed potatoes
1 egg
1 T. grated onion
2 T. melted butter

Thaw, drain, and press the spinach to remove excess moisture. Drain the salmon and clams. Beat the 2 eggs slightly, then mix with the seafood, milk, spinach, and seasonings. Spread in a buttered baking dish or pan. Make the mashed potatoes from a mix according to directions for making 2 cups, then mix in the onion and egg. Spread the potatoes over the seafood mixture and drizzle with melted butter. Bake 25 minutes at 350°, cut into 4 portions, and serve.

●●●●

Surprise Ingredient Seafood Salad

Nobody will guess that this creamy salad contains an entire loaf of bread to stretch out a meager catch.

1 loaf day-old sandwich bread
4 hardboiled eggs
Big sweet onion, minced
1 lb. mixed, cooked seafood (shrimp, fish, crab, lobster, clams)
1 c. celery, finely diced
3 c. light mayonnaise

Cut the crusts off the bread and strew them for the birds. Cut the bread into small cubes and pile them into a big mixing bowl. Add the diced eggs, onion, drained and broken-up seafood, celery, and mayo. Refrigerate overnight and you'll find that the bread has disappeared, creating a creamy and flavorful seafood salad. Serve it in lettuce cups or green pepper halves with lots of seasonal fresh vegetables and crisp crackers.

●●●●

Brown Rice Seafood Salad Supreme

This is another make-ahead summer salad that I like to have ready in the refrigerator for a quick lunch, grabbed at a roadside rest stop when we're in a hurry to make a distant campsite before nightfall. Or, serve it for dinner. It's filling and meaty yet very low in fat.

½ lb. shrimp, cooked, shelled,
  and deveined
½ lb. bay scallops, cooked
2 c. cooked brown rice
½ c. julienne strips sweet pepper
½ c. cooked peas
¼ c. sunflower seeds
¼ c. raisins
1 c. Jarlsberg cheese, in
  julienne strips

Greens for garnish
Dressing:
1 c. plain yogurt
½ c. cucumber, chopped
  and seeded
½ c. chopped green onion
3 T. lemon juice
2 T. light soy sauce
Dash lemon pepper

Combine the dressing ingredients and set aside. Combine the salad ingredients, add dressing, and chill. To serve, arrange greens on 4–6 plates and spoon salad on them. Serve with crispbread, sweet butter, and, for dessert, thin slices of melon garnished with gjetost cheese. Pronounced YAY-tossed, this sweet, caramel-like cheese, served with plain crackers and a juicy fruit, makes a quick but chic dessert.

●●●●

CHAPTER TEN

Some Like It in One Pot: One-Dish Meals

Unlike recipes that are served over rice or noodles, or that ask you to cook a pasta separately or otherwise juggle burners and wash more than one pot, these are made completely in one pan or casserole. Each is a complete meal.

Garbanzo Bonanza

This dish carries well and improves with reheating. Make it ahead at home and carry in a casserole to reheat in the microwave or in boilable bags to heat atop the stove.

1 lb. hot or mild Italian sausage
Lg. onion, diced
3 large cloves garlic, mashed
2-lb. can stewed tomatoes
2 t. mixed Italian herbs
2 c. water

1 lb. macaroni
1-lb. can garbanzo beans
Salt, pepper
Fresh parsley
Freshly grated Parmesan cheese

Cut the sausage into small pieces and sizzle it with the garlic and onion until it loses its pink color. Pour off any excess fat. Add tomatoes, herbs, and water and bring to a boil. Add raw macaroni and cook over high heat until it's tender. Reduce heat. Drain garbanzos and add them, then heat thoroughly. Add salt and pepper to taste, stir in a handful of freshly snipped parsley, and serve in shallow soup plates with lots of garlic bread and a green salad with zesty Italian dressing. Pass the Parmesan cheese to be added to individual taste.

●●●●

Presto Pizza

Courtesy of Alaska Canned Salmon, the California Pistachio Commission, and Norseland Foods, this pizza throws together, right in the pan, in minutes. Pesto sauce is found in the refrigerated section of the supermarket (with the fresh pastas and sauces). Or use your own favorite pesto recipe.

1 tube prepared pizza dough (12-inch crust)
¾ to 1 c. prepared pesto sauce
3 c. shredded Jarlsberg cheese
1 c. coarsely chopped natural California pistachios
7½-oz. can Alaska salmon, drained and flaked

Arrange pizza dough in a 15 X 10 X ¾-inch pan or a 12-inch pizza pan. Spread with pesto sauce. Sprinkle with cheese, pistachios, and salmon. Bake at 425° for 15–17 minutes or until crust is golden. As a main dish, this goes well with a garnish of chilled cranberry sauce, soft bread sticks, and crunchy raw vegetables, followed by a tart, lemony dessert.

●●●●

Pizza as You Like It

Keep on hand a supply of prebaked pizza crusts and vacuum-packaged grated mozzarella cheese. Both are

one-dish meals

labeled with expiration dates but have fairly long shelf lives. Then use your imagination to create instant pizzas whenever you like. Simply bake any of these at 400° until they're heated through and the mozzarella is bubbly. Suggested fillings:

- A can of black beans, drained, sprinkled with half a packet of taco seasoning, chopped sweet onion, diced fresh tomatoes, and chopped parsley or cilantro. Top with mozzarella or jack cheese.
- Leftover vegetables such as broccoli florets, cauliflower bits, and snipped green beans scattered atop a crust spread lightly with softened cream cheese. Sprinkle with dried basil and drizzle with pizza sauce. Top with mozzarella and bake.
- Canned chunk chicken, sliced water chestnuts, and chunk pineapple, topped with mozzarella. Bake until melted.
- Paper-thin slices of lox, tomato, and Bermuda onion arranged in overlapping profusion atop a crust spread with sour cream. Top with mozzarella. Bake to melt cheese.
- Sliced hardboiled eggs sprinkled with crumbled, cooked bacon and shredded mozzarella, then baked.
- A small can of corned beef, pulled apart, plus a 16-oz. can of sauerkraut, well drained. Top with mozzarella or shredded Swiss cheese before baking.
- Imitation crab meat and canned Newburg sauce. Splash with sherry and top with mozzarella. Bake as for pizza.

●●●●

Chili Casserole

16-oz. can chili without beans
16-oz. can kidney beans
16-oz. can stewed tomatoes, Mexican style
12-oz. can Mexicorn
1 pkg. cornbread mix
1 egg
Water
Grated jack cheese (optional)

This is the simplest one-dish meal in the world, but it's colorful, complete, and will warm your jacket in the coldest autumn winds. Simply dump the undrained chili, beans, and tomatoes into a roomy saucepan, and heat it. Meanwhile, empty the cornbread mix into a plastic bag and add the juice from the Mexicorn, about half the corn, the egg, and enough water to make a thick batter. Blend only until it's evenly moistened. Stir the remaining corn into the chili. When the chili mixture comes to a boil, drizzle the batter over it, cover, lower heat, and simmer just until the cornbread is set. Ladle into bowls and serve with big, crunchy celery sticks. Pass the grated cheese and a bottle of Tabasco separately and plan a quenching dessert such as coffee laced with Grand Marnier.

●●●●

Cock-a-Leekie Casserole

4 big, meaty chicken thighs
2 T. oil
2 leeks
2 c. water
2 chicken bouillon cubes
2 T. instant-blend flour
1 c. pitted prunes, cut up
Salt, pepper to taste

Brown the chicken in the oil and drain off excess fat. Cut up and add the white portion of the leeks, plus the water and bouillon cubes. Cover and simmer until the meat is very tender, then add the prunes, sprinkle in the flour, boil to thicken, and season to taste. Serve in bowls or soup plates, with slabs of French bread to soak in the gravy. Add a side salad of mixed greens, sliced radishes, and grated carrots with a poppy seed dressing, and a colorful dessert such as baked apples sauced with cherry yogurt.

●●●●

Cassoulet

1 lb. sweet Italian sausage	2 lg. onions
3 lbs. lamb for stew	1 can ready-to-use
3 cans Great Northern	beef broth
or other white beans	2 T. instant-blend flour
1 lb. carrots	Salt, pepper, thyme
4 ribs celery	

Cut the sausage into chunks. In a big Dutch oven, frazzle the sausage and lamb over high heat until they are browned. Pour off excess fat. Add the vegetables and broth, cover, and simmer over a low-medium flame until the lamb is tender. Make a paste with the flour and a little water and add it. Boil to thicken, thin with water or red wine if necessary to make a soupy stew, then season to taste. Serve in soup plates, with lots of French bread. Serves 8–12.

Put leftovers in a boilable bag to reheat without having to wash a pot.

●●●●

Brunswick Stew

Let this simmer on the galley stove all afternoon on a chilly day or use a pressure cooker to speed cooking. The meat must fall apart into shreds. This makes a huge batch that will serve 12–20, so it's great for campground potluck suppers.

2 lbs. chicken thighs, skinned	4 cans, 1 lb. each, cream-style corn
2 lbs. lean chuck	16-oz. can green limas
2 lbs. lean pork	3 T. vinegar
8 c. water	1 T. dried sage
3 lg. onions, diced	Salt, pepper
46-oz. can tomato juice	Hot sauce to taste

Choose very lean beef and pork roasts and have the butcher grind them coarsely. Bring the meats, water, and onion to a boil in a large, heavy kettle over a high flame. Reduce heat, cover, and simmer until meats are very tender. Remove the thighs with tongs, discard the bones, and chop the meat. Return chicken to the stew with the remaining ingredients, and cook over medium heat, stirring often to prevent scorching, until it's well heated. Serve in soup bowls with a hearty whole-wheat bread, apple butter, raw vegetable sticks, and ginger-bread with vanilla sauce for dessert.

●●●●

Lamb Shanks

4 lamb shanks, trimmed of excess fat	8 dried apricot halves
Flour, salt, pepper	8 pitted prunes
2–3 T. oil	16-oz. can potatoes
2 lg. onions, diced	16-oz. can whole baby
¼ t. cinnamon	carrots

Dredge the lamb in seasoned flour and brown it in the oil. Cover with water, bring to a boil, cover, and simmer until the lamb is almost tender. Add the prunes, apricots, onions, and cinnamon and simmer until everything is tender, adding more water if necessary. Drain, rinse, and drain the potatoes and add them, along with the drained carrots. Heat through, then serve with a lime jello salad, a rich challah loaf, and a dessert such as pop-sicles to be eaten during an after-dinner stroll. Serves 4.

●●●●

One-Step Casserole

This is one to use with the meat/onion/green pepper mixture that so many of us cook ahead of time at home in huge batches and freeze in meal-size por-

tions for camping trips. The same meat mixture is the basis for many family favorites including chili and spaghetti sauce. Traditionalists prefer lean ground beef, sometimes with some ground veal and ground pork added. Modern cooks use all or part ground turkey.

2½ c. cooked ground meat/onion/green pepper mix	2-lb. can tomatoes
	1½ c. water
	8-oz. bag wide noodles
Salt, pepper	8-oz. pkg. shredded cheese
15-oz. can tomato sauce	

Sprinkle the *uncooked* noodles in the baking pan and top with the cooked meat mixture, seasonings, tomatoes and tomato sauce, and water. Cover with foil and bake for 45 minutes at 350°. Remove from the oven, take off the foil, add the cheese, and bake a few minutes more until the cheese melts. Let stand 10 minutes and serve with Italian bread and a leafy salad.

●●●●

First Night in Camp Casserole

Assemble this all-in-one meal at home and carry it in the refrigerator. While you travel, flavors blend and the macaroni "cooks" itself.

2 c. milk	2 cans, 6½ oz. each, chunk chicken
2 cans condensed cream of mushroom soup	6 oz. grated cheddar
	Med. onion, finely chopped
8-oz. pkg. macaroni	½ bell pepper, finely diced
6½-oz. can water chestnuts	Handful fresh parsley, minced

Whisk together the milk and soup to make a smooth sauce. Arrange the remaining ingredients evenly in a buttered 3-quart bake-and-serve casserole and cover with the milk mixture. Cover and refrigerate for at least 8 hours. Bake covered casserole at 350° for about 75 minutes, remove from oven, and let stand 10 minutes before serving. If you've brought split and buttered rolls, a bag of washed and cut-up celery and carrot sticks, and a bag of Tootsie Pops for dessert, your first night's meal is complete, with hardly a glance at the galley.

●●●●

Ham and Broccoli Bake

2 (10-oz.) pkgs. frozen chopped broccoli
1 lb. canned ham, diced
6 oz. sharp cheddar, shredded
3 c. milk
4 eggs
2 c. biscuit mix
½ t. dried thyme

Thaw the broccoli and spread it in a buttered 13 X 9-inch casserole. Top with the ham and cheese. Put in a 350° oven while you beat the milk and eggs together, then beat in biscuit mix just until it's moistened evenly. Pour evenly over the ham mixture and drift with thyme. Bake at 350° for about 50 minutes, or until the topping is golden brown.

●●●●

Pasta Fazuli

Although there are countless versions and various spellings of this filling favorite, this is one of the many "right" ways to prepare a versatile one-dish classic. Make it two to three days ahead to warm up aboard, or throw it together in the galley in minutes.

1 lb. sweet Italian sausage
Lg. onion, diced
2–3 ribs celery, diced
3 cloves garlic, minced
16-oz. can chicken broth

16-oz. can Great Northern beans
1½ cups water
1 c. uncooked macaroni
½ c. freshly grated Romano cheese

If the sausage is in casings, remove them. Break up and brown the sausage in a large skillet with the vegetables. Drain off excess fat. Add the chicken broth, water, and the beans with their liquid; bring to a boil; add macaroni and simmer, covered, over very low flame until the macaroni is tender and moisture is absorbed. Add salt to taste (optional). Fold in the cheese just before serving or sprinkle it atop each serving. Add a green salad with Italian dressing and an Italian loaf, thickly sliced, to make a banquet for 4.

••••

Chili Under a Blanket

Get out your largest kettle, preferably one that can go directly from stove to table. A large skillet or Dutch oven is best, because it is large enough in diameter to accommodate the dozen biscuits that form the warm blanket that turns this into a one-dish feast.

3 lbs. ground turkey	1½ c. water
3 lg. onions, diced	2 beef bouillon cubes
3–5 cloves garlic, minced	(or 2 t. bouillon granules)
2 lg. carrots, diced	2 T. sweet paprika
2 bell peppers, diced	2 T. mixed Italian herbs
2 jalapeño peppers,	1 T. ground cumin
seeded and diced	20-oz. can kidney beans
15-oz. can tomato sauce	Salt, pepper if needed

Brown the turkey, using a little oil if necessary, with the vegetables. Add the remaining ingredients, cover, and simmer until everything is tender and flavorful.

Meanwhile, make up the biscuit topping:

3 c. biscuit mix
16-oz. container plain yogurt
12 oz. shredded jack cheese
2–3 dashes hot sauce

Mix the biscuit mix and yogurt, adding a little extra milk if necessary, to make a thick dough. Fold in the cheese and turn out the mixture on a floured dishtowel to knead only briefly, to blend well. Pat dough to a circle about ½ inch thick, and cut in quarters, then thirds, to form 12 wedges. Bake these on a lightly greased baking sheet for 15 minutes, or until golden brown, at 425°. Arrange the biscuits atop the hot chili and take it to the table. You can now spoon out 12 zesty servings, ladling the juicy chili over and under the crusty biscuits.

Complete the meal with individual dishes of a firefighter salad such as lime gel with grated carrots, then haul the watermelon out of the creek where it has been cooling and serve it in big, juicy wedges.

●●●●

Tunasagne (rhymes with Lasagne)

6 no-cook lasagne noodles
1 c. frozen peas, thawed
8-oz. can diced carrots
12½-oz. can tuna
1 c. ricotta cheese
2 eggs
12-oz. pkg. grated mozzarella
¼ c. freshly grated Parmesan cheese

Dip the noodles in hot water according to package directions and arrange 3 in a greased 12 X 7-inch casserole. Sprinkle with the peas, drained carrots, and drained tuna. Whisk the eggs into the ricotta cheese and spread over the tuna mixture. Sprinkle with half the mozzarella cheese. Dip the remaining noodles and arrange them atop the casserole. Sprinkle with the remaining mozzarella, then with the Parmesan. Bake at 350° for about 30 minutes or until the cheeses are melted and the filling set. Complete the meal with toasted garlic bread and gallons of green salad, and pass out individual bags of jellybeans, in each person's favorite flavor or color, to munch while you play a twilight game of frisbee.

Variation: Proceed as above, substituting 12 ounces of finely diced, cooked ham for the tuna, and a dozen lightly steamed asparagus spears for the vegetables. All lasagnes cut more easily if they're allowed to stand 5–10 minutes. This one, because of the fresh asparagus (canned asparagus can be used but doesn't give the same fresh, garden taste), cuts better with a serrated knife.

●●●●

Pizza Puff

If you're using a ground-meat mixture you made in advance at home, substitute 3 cups of it for the ground meat, onion, garlic, and green pepper, and put it directly into the baking dish. Stir in the spaghetti sauce mix, tomato sauce, and water and proceed.

1 lb. ground beef or turkey
Lg. onion, diced
2 cloves garlic, minced
Bell pepper, diced
1½-oz. packet spaghetti
    sauce mix
15-oz. can tomato sauce
½ c. water

8-oz. package shredded
    mozzarella cheese
2 eggs
1 c. milk
1 c. flour
2 oz. Parmesan cheese,
    freshly grated (about ½ c.)

Brown the meat and vegetables together, pour off excess fat, and add the spaghetti sauce mix, tomato sauce, and water. Turn the mixture into a large, deep pie dish or a 9 X 13-inch baking pan. Sprinkle with the mozzarella. Whisk together the eggs, milk, and flour and pour over the dish, then sprinkle with the Parmesan and bake at 400° for about 30 minutes or until golden brown. The batter will puff up around the meat, forming its own crust. Cut and serve at once. Serves 8.

●●●●

Stovetop Rice Pizza

For this you'll need a roomy, nonstick, 12-inch skillet. It's a way to make pizza without having to raise dough, and it uses up leftover rice.

3 c. cooked rice
2 eggs, beaten
6-oz. jar sliced mushrooms
Pepperoni as desired
8-oz. can tomato sauce
1 t. mixed Italian herbs
Other toppings, ad lib
6-oz. pkg. shredded mozzarella cheese

Stir the eggs into the rice and press around the bottom and sides of a cold, lightly greased, nonstick skillet to form a crust. Cover and cook over medium flame until the egg begins to set. Top with mushrooms, pepperoni, any other favorite toppings, and then the tomato sauce. Sprinkle with Italian herbs, then with the cheese. Cover and continue cooking over low-medium flame until the cheese is melted and crust is set. Serves 4.

To serve it from the pan, use a non-metal cutter that won't damage the nonstick finish. Divide into wedges and serve on plates. This is best eaten with knife and fork, not from the hand like yeast-dough pizzas.

●●●●

One Potato, Two: Starches Aside

If you're like many RV campers, you make many a meal out of meat from the grill, a starch side dish, and a big salad. With a broiled chop or burger these recipes are basic meal makers.

Bread Salad

This is not only a quick and easy starch side dish with a plain meat, it's a good way to use stale bread on those trips when you've brought too much.

1 loaf stale French bread
2 firm, ripe tomatoes, diced
¼ c. sunflower nuts
Small sweet onion, diced
1 T. minced fresh parsley
⅓ c. Italian dressing

Cut the bread into ½-inch cubes and let it air dry. Toss together with the rest of the ingredients and serve at once. If you don't have fresh parsley, use a sprinkling of dill. Dried parsley doesn't have enough zest for this dish.

●●●●

> Boil quartered red potatoes just until tender and marinate in a vinaigrette dressing overnight, adding chunks of cucumbers, celery, sweet pepper, and other raw vegetables if you like. Thread on skewers and serve as a cold potato salad-on-a-stick.

Sauerkraut Noodle Skillet

This recipe was developed by the National Kraut Packers Association. It's a tangy side dish to serve with grilled pork chops or baked ham, but it's robust enough to serve as a main dish for a light supper. If you make it ahead at home to warm up in the microwave, the flavor will be more tangy and better developed.

1 T. vegetable oil	1 t. caraway seeds
Med. onion, sliced	1 c. chicken broth
1½ c. sliced mushrooms	1 c. plain yogurt
2 c. sauerkraut, rinsed and drained	½ c. part skim ricotta cheese
1 T. sweet paprika	6 oz. medium egg noodles
2 t. flour	(about 3 c.)

Sauté the onions and mushrooms in the oil in a large skillet. Stir in the kraut. Sprinkle the flour, paprika, and caraway over the mixture, then stir in the broth and simmer 25 minutes. Whisk the ricotta and yogurt together and add to the sauerkraut mixture. Heat but do not boil. Cook and drain the noodles, and toss them with the sauerkraut mixture.

●●●●

Savory Rice Salad

On a hot night have this ready in the refrigerator to serve with any meat hot from the campsite's barbecue grill. It serves as a starch and salad in one. Add a bouquet of grilled vegetables to complete the plate.

2 T. white wine vinegar
1 T. olive oil
¼ t. each salt, sugar, pepper
2 c. warm rice
2 T. sliced scallions
1 c. chopped tomato
3 oz. Saga garlic-chive cheese, rind on, cut up
⅓ c. sliced olives

Stir the vinegar, oil, salt, sugar, and pepper together and pour them over the rice. Stir to mix completely, then stir in the scallions. Chill, covered, and stir in tomato, cheese, and olives just before serving. Serves 4.

●●●●

Pasta à la Grecque

The word orzo means barley, yet like other pastas it's made from wheat. Because of its small size and rice-like shape, it is easy to toast first in butter, giving it a rich and nutty taste.

2 T. butter
1 clove garlic, finely chopped
1½ c. orzo macaroni
1 envelope onion-mushroom soup mix
3¼ c. water
6 oz. mushrooms, sliced
¼ c. chopped parsley

In a 3-quart saucepan melt the butter over medium-high heat and cook the garlic with the orzo, stirring constantly, until golden. Stir in the soup mix and water. Bring to a boil, cover, and simmer 10 minutes. Add mushrooms but do not stir. Simmer, covered, 10 minutes more. Stir in parsley, remove from heat, and let stand 10–15 minutes while remaining liquid is absorbed. Serves 6–8.

●●●●

Green Rice Casserole

Anytime you can combine a starch and a vegetable or two in a rich, creamy, colorful casserole, you save time and dishwashing. This casserole goes well with grilled chicken, or it can stand alone as a vegetarian main dish. Assemble the casserole at home and keep it cold to bake on the first night out.

2 T. butter	1½ c. milk
1 bunch fresh broccoli, cut up	2 c. cooked brown rice
Small onion, diced	4 oz. cheddar cheese, grated
3 T. instant-blend flour	⅓ c. seasoned bread crumbs
1 t. prepared mustard	Bits of butter (optional)

Melt the butter and sauté the broccoli pieces and onion until they are crisp-tender. Stir in the flour and mustard, then continue stirring over low flame while adding the milk. Add the rice and cheese and put into a buttered casserole. Top with the bread crumbs and dot with butter. Bake at 350° until heated through.

●●●●

Oven Fries

2 lg. baking potatoes (total 1 lb.)
1 egg white
½ c. grated Parmesan cheese and
2 t. oregano, blended

Scrub the potatoes and cut them lengthwise into 8 wedges each. Beat the egg white until foamy. Dip the potatoes into the egg white, then the cheese. Bake on a well-greased baking sheet at 425° for 25 minutes, or until golden on the outside and tender inside. Serves 4.

●●●●

Mashed Potato Pie

One of the shortcuts I use in RV cooking is instant mashed potatoes, but, to be honest, they need a little help before they can pass muster. Here's one way to disguise them. The result is a twice-baked potato in a flaky crust.

1 deep-dish pie crust
6 servings instant potatoes
2 eggs, beaten
⅓ c. grated Parmesan cheese
½ c. yogurt or sour cream

Bake the pie crust at 450° for 5 minutes, then set aside. Make up the potatoes according to directions on the box, then stir in the remaining ingredients and spread in the pie shell. Bake at 425° until the crust is brown and the filling set, about 30–40 minutes. Let stand 5 minutes, then serve in wedges. Serves 6–8.

••••

Four-Vegetable Risotto

Have you tried the new Dilijan liquid spices? They're ideal for RV camping because they keep better than dried.

10-oz. pkg. spinach, thawed
and well drained
14½-oz. can chicken broth
1½ c. rice
½ t. liquid garlic
1 c. diced onion

¼ t. liquid hot pepper
½ t. liquid oregano
⅓ c. freshly grated Parmesan
½ c. thinly sliced carrot
½ c. thinly sliced celery
3 T. butter

Thaw the spinach and press out excess moisture. Add water to the chicken broth to make 2½ cups. Combine liquid spices and cheese and set aside. Melt the butter in a roomy saucepan and sauté the rice and onion. Add broth, spinach, celery, and carrots, bring to a boil, cover, reduce heat, and simmer 20 minutes. Stir in cheese and spice mixture, cover again, and let stand 5 minutes more. Serves 6.

●●●●

Wild Rice Stovetop Dressing

6-oz. box rice and wild rice mix
1 c. orange juice
1½ c. water
2 T. butter
1 T. fresh orange zest
½ c. pecans

Sauté the rice in the butter until it's brown, then stir in the seasoning packet, water, orange juice, and orange zest. Bring to a boil, cover, reduce heat, and simmer until the liquid is absorbed, about 25 minutes. Stir in the pecans just before serving. Serve with chicken or pork.

Note: This is delicious when made with regular, shelled pecans, and better still when made with toasted, salted pecans.

●●●●

Bring a big pot of water to a boil and cook, in the same water, noodles plus boil-in-the-bag creamed spinach. Drain the noodles and stir in the spinach with a nugget of butter and a hefty dose of grated Romano.

Oven-broasted Potatoes

Although it calls for only three ingredients, this recipe is an entire symphony of meaty, crusty flavors. It goes especially well with steak or hamburgers from the outdoor grill.

2 lbs. small red potatoes, scrubbed and quartered
1 packet Lipton onion soup mix
⅓ c. virgin olive oil

Put the potatoes in a zip-top plastic bag and add the soup mix and oil, then zip the bag closed and toss until the potatoes are well coated. Turn out the potatoes onto a lightly oiled shallow cooking pan or casserole and bake at 450°, stirring occasionally, 40 minutes or until crispy on the outside and tender inside. Serves 6–8.

●●●●

Potatoes Fan-tastic

6 Idaho potatoes, peeled
½ stick butter
¾ c. water
1 t. chicken bouillon granules
Freshly ground pepper
⅓ c. bread crumbs
3 T. freshly grated Parmesan

Put the potatoes on a cutting board and cut them into ⅛-inch slices without cutting all the way through the bottom. Slices will fan out slightly. Stir the bouillon granules into the water. Place the potatoes in a greased, shallow baking pan and pour the chicken bouillon over them. Melt the butter and pour about half of it over the potatoes. Bake 30 minutes at 375°, then sprinkle with the bread crumbs and drizzle with the remaining butter.

Bake another 10–15 minutes or until the potatoes are tender, then sprinkle with the grated cheese and serve.

••••

Turnip Patch Potatoes

1 lb. potatoes, peeled and sliced
1 lb. turnips, peeled and sliced
1 clove garlic
3 T. butter
Salt, freshly ground pepper

½ t. nutmeg
1 c. grated cheese, preferably
  Swiss or Gruyère
Small can (⅔ c.) evaporated milk
⅓ c. bread crumbs

Boil the potatoes and turnips together until just tender and drain them. Spray a 1½-quart casserole with nonstick spray, and rub with garlic. Alternate layers of the vegetables with the grated cheese and bits of the butter. Sprinkle with nutmeg and pour the milk over all. Top with the bread crumbs and more bits of butter. Bake at 400° until it's bubbling and tender, with a butter-crusted top. Serves 5–6.

••••

Garlicky Grits

If you haven't yet discovered grits as an alternative to potatoes, now is the time.

1 c. regular grits, uncooked
1 stick butter
6-oz. pkg. shredded cheddar
2 cloves garlic, minced
2 eggs
Milk

Cook the grits according to directions on the package. When they're done, turn off the flame and stir in the butter, garlic, and cheese. Break the eggs into a measuring cup, then add milk to make 1 cup. Beat the eggs and milk, then stir in the grits. Turn into a greased casserole and bake 45 minutes at 350°.

●●●●

Saffron Rice

There is no substitute for saffron, which is very expensive but worth the splurge when you want a special rice dish to accompany that once-in-a-lifetime catch of fresh salmon or walleye.

Med. onion, diced
1 stick butter
1¼ c. long-grain rice
¼ c. white wine or white grape juice
¼ t. saffron threads
Small can mushroom slices, drained
2 c. water
2 t. chicken bouillon granules
⅓ c. thawed green peas

Sauté the onions in some of the butter until they're translucent, then add the rice and remaining butter and stir to coat until the rice, too, looks translucent. Add the wine and bring to a boil. Then add the water, bouillon, mushrooms, and saffron and return to a boil. Cover and simmer over very low heat, or in a covered casserole in a 350° oven, for 20 minutes. Stir in the green peas and serve.

●●●●

Calypso Beans 'n Rice

Almost every island in the Caribbean has its own version of beans and rice. All that varies is the type of bean and the degree of hotness. For the beans use black (turtle) beans, kidney beans, pigeon peas, pinto or red beans. Navy beans or limas are not used in these dishes.

1 lb. can beans, drained
3 c. water
16-oz. can coconut milk (not cream of coconut)
2 c. raw rice
2 cloves garlic, minced
½ t. dried thyme
1 t. tomato paste (optional)
Salt, pepper, hot sauce to taste

What could be easier? Simply combine everything in a roomy, heavy, lidded pot, bring to a boil, reduce the heat, and simmer until all the liquid is absorbed. With regular, long-grain rice this takes 20–25 minutes. Stir and serve, with additional hot sauce on the side if you like. Serves 4–6 as a main dish, 8–10 as a side dish.

●●●●

Shamrock Rice

2 c. hot, cooked rice
½ c. minced parsley
3 scallions, including green part, thinly sliced
Grated zest of one med. lime

Fold the parsley, scallions, and lime zest lightly into hot rice, salt to taste, and serve with fish or chicken. Serves 5–6.

●●●●

Yorkshire Pudding

It's really just a great big popover. The ingredients whisk together in seconds, yet this puffs up to make an impressive starch dish that everybody loves. In England it is made with a roast, right in the meat drippings, but by using butter instead you can make it anytime to serve with any meat.

3 T. butter
1 c. flour
1 c. milk
1 t. salt
2 eggs

Heat the oven to 400° and melt the butter in a 10-inch round pie plate or an 8 X 10-inch casserole. Swirl the butter around to coat the bottom and sides thoroughly. Whisk the flour, milk, salt, and eggs together just until smooth and pour into the hot, melted butter. Bake 30 minutes or until golden and puffy, then race it to the table before it collapses.

●●●●

Stuffing Stuffed Tomatoes

When tomatoes are ripe and seasonal, buy them by the bushel along the roadside and splurge on this colorful side dish with any meat.

Tomatoes
Stovetop dressing

Slice off the tops of meaty, ripe tomatoes and scoop out the insides. Discard the seeds and watery pulp. If necessary, take a tiny slice off the bottom of each tomato so they can stand upright in a baking pan. Now stir up a package of stovetop dressing according to package directions, or use your own recipe, and pile it loosely into the tomato shells. Bake at 350° for 15–20 minutes or until heated through and browned on top. Plan one per person, with a few extras for hefty eaters.

Variations: Try this with any type of stuffing—rice, cornbread, wild rice, or even your favorite oyster stuffing.

••••

Baked Bulgur

3 T. butter
1 c. bulgur (parboiled whole wheat)
Med. onion, diced
2–3 ribs celery, diced
2 c. water
2 t. chicken bouillon granules

Melt the butter in a heavy saucepan and sauté the bulgur with the vegetables. Add the water and bouillon, bring to a boil, cover, reduce heat, and simmer 15 minutes. Let stand off the heat for a few minutes, then fluff with a fork and serve. Makes 6–8 servings.

••••

Tabouli

Once you discover the ease of cooking with bulgur, which is an ancient version of precooked "fast" food, you'll want to try it in many recipes or as a hot breakfast cereal. Tabouli is a Middle Eastern starch dish that utilizes this wheat without cooking. It's best if made ahead and chilled thoroughly.

1 c. bulgur
1 c. boiling water
1 clove garlic
3–4 scallions, finely sliced
1 c. freshly chopped parsley
  (leaves from 1 bunch)
2 tomatoes, seeded and diced

2¼-oz. can sliced ripe olives,
  drained
¼ c. virgin olive oil
⅓ c. lemon juice
1 t. salt
½ t. mixed Italian herbs

Place the bulgur and garlic in a large bowl, stir in the boiling water, and let it stand for 30 minutes. Discard garlic. Fold in the remaining vegetables. Shake the oil and lemon juice together with the salt and herbs and toss with the mixture. Cover and chill. Serve it with cold cuts, meat hot from the grill, or a roast. Serves 6–8.

Variation: To make this a meaty, main-dish salad, fold in a can of well-drained garbanzo beans.

••••

Hashbrown Hustle

2-lb. package frozen hash brown potatoes, thawed
Small onion, finely diced
1 can cream of celery soup
16-oz. container sour cream
10-oz. pkg. shredded cheddar
½ stick butter, melted
1½ c. crushed cornflakes

Butter a 3-quart casserole. Mix together everything but the butter and cornflake crumbs, and pile into the casserole. Sprinkle with the crumbs and drizzle with the butter. Bake 1 hour at 350°.

Note: For messless mixing, moosh everything (except the butter and crumbs) together in an extra large food storage bag, and strip it out into the casserole. Throw the bag away.

●●●●

Barbecued Potatoes

Layer sliced onions and potatoes in a heavily buttered casserole, at a ratio of one onion for each two potatoes. Drizzle each layer lightly with your favorite barbecue sauce. Cover and bake at 350° for 45 minutes or until vegetables are tender. Then uncover, add more barbecue sauce, and bake 15 minutes more. This can also be made on the grill, sealed tightly in heavy-duty aluminum foil.

●●●●

Fast Lane

•Make your own prepackaged rice pilaf mix at home. Into each zip-top sandwich bag put ingredients for one batch. They include rice, chicken or beef bouillon granules, raisins, curry powder, and dried onion.

•Experiment with different rices, not just white and brown but long and short grain, arborio, and aromatic. Each produces a different result, giving simple meals more variety.

•Dress up deli potato salad by adding caraway seeds, sliced scallions, sliced radishes, diced sweet pepper and tomato, sliced stuffed olives, or a seeded, diced cucumber.

•To toast rice, spread raw kernels of regular, long grain rice in a shallow pan and bake 15–20 minutes, or until golden, at 350°. Boil as usual.

•To make a serving of sticky rice look more festive, serve it with an ice cream scoop.

Slow Cookery and
Rainy-Day Fare

Although simple, snappy meals are often thought to be the main-stay of RV cooks, there are times when you want carefree meals that will cook themselves in a slow oven or a crockpot while you and the family play the day away.

These recipes can be cooked in a Dutch oven buried in the coals of a campfire, in an oven, or in an electric crock cooker. The secret to all slow cooking is to keep foods heavily lidded or wrapped, at low heat. Try not to peek; heat and moisture will escape.

Temperatures given are for electric cookers at 1-2-3-4-5 or Low, Medium, and High. To use an oven, cook these meals at 275° for Low, 300° for Medium, or 325° for High. To cook in a campfire, use well-started coals from a "feeding" fire to keep the pot smothered in steady heat.

A warning: I don't recommend cooking underway, either in an oven or an electric cooker. Any flame is a hazard on the road and, in a tight turn or a panic stop, doors can open or lids fly off. These recipes are intended for use in camp on days when you want the meal to cook itself, even if it takes all day.

Corned Beef in Beer

4–5 onions
12-oz. can beer
4–5 lb. round of corned beef, well trimmed of fat

Peel and slice the onions and layer them in the bottom of a Dutch oven or slow cooker. Add the corned beef and beer. Cover and cook on Medium-Low for 8–10 hours. To serve, remove the corned beef to a cutting board and slice across the grain. Pass the onion-beer sauce, slabs of rye bread, sweet butter, and big dill pickles. If you want additional vegetables, boil potatoes and carrots together in one big pot and slather them with butter and a sprinkling of caraway seed.

••••

Barbecued Ribs

This recipe is courtesy of West Bend, maker of several sizes and styles of electric slow cookers.

4 lbs. lean country-style pork ribs
10½-oz. can condensed tomato soup
½ c. cider vinegar
½ c. brown sugar
1 T. soy sauce
1 t. celery seed
1 t. chili powder

Trim off excess fat and place ribs in the cooking pot. Combine the remaining ingredients and pour over the ribs. Cook at Setting #3/Medium for 7–8 hours, or #5/High for 3–4 hours. It's a meal for paper plates and fingers. Eat it with torn chunks of Italian bread to mop up the sauce, cole slaw, corn on the cob, and spears of fresh pineapple, followed by generous portions of pre-moistened towelettes. Serves 4.

●●●●

Stuffed Cabbage

Lg. cabbage
1 lb. lean ground beef
1 t. salt
½ t. pepper
⅔ c. raw white rice
Small onion, chopped
16-oz. can tomatoes
8-oz. can tomato sauce

Core cabbage and place core side down in a few inches of boiling water for a few minutes to wilt leaves. Remove 8 outer leaves and coarsely chop remaining cabbage. Mix ground beef, salt, pepper, rice, and onion and divide into 8 portions. Place one portion on each cabbage leaf and roll up.

The recipe can be assembled up to this point at home and stored in the refrigerator in a heavy plastic bag. Do not freeze. To proceed, put the chopped cabbage in the bottom of the cooker and top with tomatoes. Arrange stuffed cabbage on top and cover. Cook 7–8 hours on #3/Medium. Serves 4.

Complete the meal with rich egg braid bread, a leafy salad, and apple tarts.

●●●●

Finnish Stew

This is a sort of Scandinavian beef bourguignonne, fork-tender and steeped in mysterious flavors. The secret is to use three different meats. With each combination, the flavor is subtly different.

4 lbs. boneless cubed meat (beef, turkey, lamb, pork, veal)
6 med. onions, sliced
2 t. whole allspice
1 T. salt

Combine all ingredients in slow cooker and cook 7–8 hours at a #3/Medium setting. Serve with new potatoes in dill and butter, limpa rye bread, and a medley of root vegetables. Serves 8–10. For dessert, try fresh raspberries with Danish butter cookies from a can.

●●●●

Mexican Stew

3 T. oil
3 lbs. turkey or pork cubes
Bunch parsley, chopped
2 shallots, chopped
½ t. each paprika, coriander, and caraway
Salt, pepper

3 onions
¼ t. ground cloves
4 cloves garlic
16-oz. can tomatoes, drained and chopped
2 ⅓ c. water (include tomato juice)
½ oz. unsweetened chocolate

Layer meat in a slow cooker with remaining ingredients except tomatoes and chocolate. Cook 7–8 hours at #3/Medium, then add tomatoes and finely cut-up chocolate. Heat to melt chocolate, then stir and serve with fluffy white rice. Add a marinated vegetable salad, Mexican cornbread, and a flan or custard for dessert. Serves 8–10.

●●●●

Fruited Lamb

1 lb. lean lamb for stew
Flour, oil for browning
1½ c. dried fruit, cut up
(apples, white and dark
raisins, apricots, peaches,
prunes)

4 T. lemon juice
¼ c. honey
1 c. orange or apple juice
½ t. apple pie spice
1 T. cornstarch

Dredge the lamb in flour and brown it in hot oil in the cooker on its highest setting. Turn heat to lowest setting and add remaining ingredients except cornstarch. Cover and cook 9–10 hours. Pour off juices and skim off fat. Add water to pan juices to make 1½ cups. Stir cornstarch into a little water, then turn cooker to its highest setting and make a sauce using the cornstarch mixture and juices. Serve with aromatic rice, pita triangles, and coarsely shredded apple-cabbage slaw, then iced watermelon for dessert.

••••

Forgotten Stew

Many versions of this forgiving stew have been published over the years, and the recipe is worth repeating here. One of its best features for the RV cook is that it throws together in one pot; the meat does not have to be browned first. In a 325° oven it will be tender in 3–4 hours; for longer cooking (up to 8–9 hours) use 275° or a #3/Medium setting.

1-lb. can stewed tomatoes
1 c. water (part red wine
if you like)
1 beef bouillon cube
2 t. dried Italian seasoning
Dash pepper
¼ c. quick-cooking tapioca

3 lbs. lean, boneless stew beef
10 carrots, peeled and diced
½ bunch celery, coarsely sliced
3 med. onions, diced
2 T. Dijon mustard
12-oz. can mushrooms
10-oz. package frozen peas

Mix everything but the mustard, mushrooms, and peas in a large Dutch oven or slow cooker. Cook on Medium/#3 or in a 275° oven for 5–7 hours. Stir in mustard, drained mushrooms, and thawed peas, salt to taste, and heat through. Serve with instant mashed potatoes, toasted garlic bread, and crunchy red apples for dessert.

●●●●

Creamy Chicken

Of all the shortcut recipes that call for condensed cream soup, this one keeps its secret best. There is something about the combination of the sherry, soup, and sour cream that makes it hard to pin down, and harder still to call the work of a lazy cook.

8 boneless chicken-breast halves
1 can cream of chicken soup
1 soup-can sherry
1 soup-can sour cream

Roll the chicken into bundles and arrange in one layer in a slow cooker or casserole. Combine the other ingredients, pour over the chicken and bake, tightly covered, 3 hours at 325° or at a #4/Medium-High setting. Serve over rice. (Variation: pound chicken breast halves flat and wrap around several leaves of dried chipped beef. Proceed as above.)

Complete the menu with fresh fruit cup, cloverleaf rolls, steamed carrots, and a dessert of canned vanilla pudding topped with finely chopped peanut butter cups.

●●●●

Slow-Lane Venison

Venison roast, about 4 lbs.
3 slices bacon
8-oz. can tomato sauce
Salt, pepper

Med. onion, diced
2 T. sugar
2 T. Worcestershire
2 T. vinegar

Place roast in a slow cooker, oven roaster, or heavy-duty foil. Lay bacon strips across the top. Combine the tomato sauce and seasonings and pour over the roast. Cover the roaster or seal the foil, and bake 4–5 hours at Medium-Low/275° or 3–4 hours at Medium/300°.

●●●●

Save for a Rainy Day

These too are recipes that take a lot of time. Bring them out on a day when you're weathered in and want to fuss around the kitchen, letting the aromas of food surround you and lift your spirits.

We've been rained in for days at a time in our RV, once during a hurricane in Nova Scotia and other times during tropical storms in Florida. During one rainy, muddy springtime in Vermont, we couldn't venture out for a week, and then only in boots and oilskins.

I set aside this separate section for a rainy day because these recipes are ideal for RV fun, even though they are not shortcut quickies. You can fuss over them, enjoying the process as much as the product.

Butter Rum Fudge

1 c. dried apricots, snipped into bits
2 c. dark brown sugar, firmly packed
1 c. white sugar
1 stick butter or oleo
1 c. half and half
7-oz. jar marshmallow cream

12-oz. package butter-scotch chips
1 c. chopped nuts
1½ t. butter-rum-vanilla flavoring*

Combine sugars, butter, and half and half in a roomy saucepan (at least 3-quart capacity) and boil, stirring, over medium heat until it forms a soft ball when a drop is placed in cold water. If you have a candy thermometer, it should read 238°. Remove from heat and stir in marshmallow, butterscotch, apricots, and flavoring. Beat well and spread in a buttered 8-inch square pan. Cool and cut into blocks.

*If you cannot find this flavoring, substitute 1 teaspoon rum flavor and ½ teaspoon vanilla.

●●●●

Popcorn Balls

First, butter everything that will come in contact with the sticky mess that will result. You'll need a pair of clean rubber or plastic gloves to protect your hands while you form the balls. Butter them too.

12 c. popped corn, "old maids" removed
1 lb. package marshmallows
½ stick butter
Optional additions:
1 c. gumdrops or
1 c. chopped nuts or
3 small candy canes, crushed, or
1 c. chocolate chips or
1 c. butterscotch chips

Put popcorn in a big, buttered container and keep it warm in a 250° oven. In a heavy pan over very low heat, or in the microwave, heat marshmallows and butter together until melted and smooth. Pour over popcorn and mix well with a buttered spoon, add any optional ingredients, and shape lightly into balls. Don't pack too tightly. Wrap individually in waxed paper.

This can also be turned into a family sculpture game if you have buttered gloves for all players. (I carry disposable plastic gloves aboard and use them for all sorts of messy tasks, from greasing wheel bearings to handling raw bacon, when water is in short supply. Strip them off and throw them away.) Instead of forming popcorn balls, have everyone make an animal, something seasonal such as a Christmas tree or a shamrock, or whatever suits their fancy. What with the shaping and trimming, the job can fill a happy hour.

●●●●

Crêpes Grand Marnier

Few foods are more versatile than crêpes, which can be filled with almost anything and served for breakfast, lunch, dinner, snacks, and desserts. The drawback is that it takes forever to make the crêpes, one at a time. A rainy day is the perfect time to stow away a stock of crêpes.

Stack them with paper toweling or waxed paper between, then refrigerate or freeze them for future use. Or make this triple batch of festive dessert crêpes. They'll keep for a couple of weeks in the refrigerator.

Crêpes:
6 eggs
2 c. milk
2 T. melted butter
1½ c. flour
2 T. sugar

Whisk together eggs and milk, stir in remaining ingredients, cover, and refrigerate 2 hours. Using a scant ¼ cup each time (you'll be making 24 crêpes), pour batter into a hot, lightly sprayed, 8-inch, nonstick skillet and tilt quickly so that batter flows around the bottom of the pan to form a thin pancake. When it's golden on the bottom, turn and cook the other side. Roll up and set aside.

Filling:
1 stick butter
1 c. sifted powdered sugar
¾ c. orange juice
¾ c. honey or light corn syrup
½ c. orange liqueur
1 orange, thinly sliced

Mix the butter and sugar, unroll crêpes, and butter each with the sugar mixture. Fold into quarters and stack in refrigerator containers in whatever size batches you can use. Combine the orange juice and syrup in a small saucepan, bring to boiling, reduce heat, and add orange slices cut into quarters. Stir in the liqueur and divide the mixture among the containers of crêpes. To serve, warm the crêpes and their syrup gently in a skillet, and spoon onto serving plates, saucing with syrup. For a flaming dessert, heat about ¼ cup orange liqueur in another small pan or skillet, pour over crêpes, and light with a match.

••••

Celebrate Vegetables

Fresh vegetables are one of travel's greatest joys. Stop at roadside stands to buy the biggest, best, and freshest of the harvest. Chayote, yucca, weirdly shaped squash, new tomato hybrids, Jerusalem artichokes, horseradish you have to grate yourself, and sweet corn more savory than can be found in any supermarket—if you don't recognize it, try it anyway, and make a new friend as the farmer tells you how to prepare it.

One of the best corn dishes we ever had was in the back woods of North Carolina, where a simple farm wife gave us a sheaf of field corn, with timid apologies, and promised us it would be good if I prepared it as she suggested. (It was heavenly.)

In the South, come to terms with the various greens harvested there. In the North, discover fiddleheads. In the Southwest, learn the many uses of prickly pear cactus, tomatillos, and blue cornmeal. Food discoveries are among travel's greatest pleasures. Vegetables, low in cost and calories, lead them all.

> Halve acorn squash, bake cut side down until tender at 350° on greased cookie sheet. Turn up, fill holes with apple pie filling from a can, and return to oven to heat through. Serve as a side dish with pork chops.

Vegetables as a Side Dish

Mystery Appetizer

Although it tastes like a feast of creamy spices, this velvety dip is made with inexpensive, low-cal eggplant. Even a heaping helping (4–5 tablespoons) is only about 50 calories. It's served as a dip with crackers or raw vegetables.

1 lb. eggplant
2 cloves garlic
2–3 scallions
2 t. vinegar
2 t. soy sauce
1 t. olive oil
¼ c. chopped parsley

Cut eggplant in half lengthwise, make a slit in each half, and slip in a peeled garlic clove. Place cut sides down on paper towel in the microwave. Bake on High 12–16 minutes or until soft. Let cool, then scoop out flesh and put in a food processor with the remaining ingredients. It's best made ahead of time at home to let flavors blend. Chill, but let it come to room temperature before serving, stir, and sprinkle with chopped parsley at the last minute.

●●●●

Stir-Fry Asparagus

1½ lbs. fresh asparagus
2 cloves garlic, mashed
3 T. peanut oil*
Salt, pepper
Hardboiled egg

Trim asparagus and cut into 1-inch-long pieces. Stir-fry garlic in oil over medium heat until softened. Careful! It burns easily. Turn heat to high and stir-fry asparagus until crisp-tender. Sprinkle with finely chopped egg.

*Because of its higher flash point, peanut oil is preferred for stir-fry dishes.

●●●●

Cabbage Casserole

With this in the oven and meat on the grill, you have a complete menu. Just add salad, hot bread, and a fruited gelatin dessert.

2 lbs. cabbage, coarsely shredded
28-oz. can tomatoes
1 t. salt
Small onion, chopped
1 clove garlic, minced
1 T. butter
1 c. raw rice, cooked (3 c.)
½ c. seasoned bread crumbs
2 oz. cheddar, grated
2 T. melted butter

Put cabbage in a saucepan with the tomatoes, chopped but undrained. Add onion and garlic and bring to a boil. Simmer, covered, 5 minutes. Add rice and salt and place in buttered casserole. Sprinkle with bread crumbs and cheese and drizzle with melted butter. Bake 45 minutes at 375°. Makes 8 side-dish servings.

●●●●

Oven-fry slabs of eggplant, green tomato, zucchini, or yellow squash after dipping in beaten egg, then seasoned cornmeal. Place on well-oiled baking sheet and bake at 450°, turning once, 30 minutes or until tender.

Crusty Potato Casserole

Lg. sweet onion, finely diced
1-lb. bag frozen hash browns
4 oz. jack cheese, grated
½ t. salt
dash pepper
1 egg, beaten
½ c. milk
2 T. butter

Combine everything in a greased casserole, ending with the butter (in bits), and bake at 350° for 20–30 minutes or until the top is lightly browned. Let stand 5 minutes before serving. Serves 4.

●●●●

Creamy Potato Casserole

6 servings instant mashed potatoes
12-oz. container creamy cottage cheese
⅓ c. sour cream
1 T. dried onion flakes
1 T. dried chives
Melted butter

Using a heavy saucepan with a tight, heavy lid, make the mashed potatoes according to package directions. Fold in the cottage cheese, sour cream, onion, and chives and drizzle with melted butter. Cover and heat in the same pan, over a very low flame, until it's hot throughout. Long, slow cooking allows the potatoes to steep and flavors to blend. For a more crusty result, bake uncovered in a buttered casserole at 350° for 30 minutes.

●●●●

Milemaker Cream Sauce, Master Recipe

Use your imagination with this sauce, varying it each time to find all the best combinations for your family's tastes. Whisk the milk and soup together, heating gently in a saucepan over low flame or in the microwave, add seasoning to taste, and spoon over hot, cooked vegetables.

1 CAN CONDENSED SOUP + ½ CUP + ¼ TO ½ t.

Cream of tomato	Milk	Basil
Cream of mushroom	Milk	Curry powder
Cream of celery	Milk	Dill weed
Cream of chicken	Milk	Thyme
Broccoli cheese	Milk	Lemon pepper

●●●●

Vegetable One-Dish Cancan

Canning doesn't improve vegetables, and in many instances it makes them almost inedible. Still, canned foods are a camping staple, and their taste can be improved. Canned potatoes taste better if drained, rinsed, and drained again. To develop the taste even further, fry in bacon fat or real butter.

Most canned vegetables taste better if served cold with a vinaigrette dressing or combined with other fresh or canned vegetables. This recipe can be thrown together in an emergency, with foods kept on your shelf, and it makes a complete accompaniment for any plain meat. It's best with freshly grated Romano or Parmesan.

Lg. onion, diced	1-lb. can sliced potatoes, drained and rinsed
Bell pepper, diced	1-lb. can stewed tomatoes
2 stalks celery, diced	1-lb. can spinach, drained
1 T. olive oil	¼ c. grated Romano or Parmesan cheese

Sauté the onion, pepper, and celery in the olive oil in a big skillet, then add the potatoes and sauté several minutes more. Add tomatoes with their juice and bring to a boil to reduce liquid slightly, then gently stir in the spinach to heat through. Sprinkle with cheese and serve.

••••

Hot and Creamy Potato Salad

2 lbs. new potatoes
⅔ c. mayonnaise
Small sweet onion, minced
1 pint cherry tomatoes, quartered
8-oz. can whole baby carrots, cut into slivers
½ jar real bacon bits

Scrub the potatoes, cut into chunks, and boil until fork tender. Drain and toss with remaining ingredients. Serve warm. Serves 6–8 as a side dish.

••••

Carrot Custard

1 lb. carrots
Small onion, diced
2 eggs
1 t. salt
dash pepper, dash nutmeg
2 T. butter, melted
1 c. milk
8 individual saltine crackers, crushed

Cook the carrots and onion together until tender, drain well, and mash. Beat in the milk, eggs, seasonings, crackers, and melted butter. If you're making this at home for baking on the go, transfer to a buttered casserole and refrigerate up to 2 days. To proceed, bake at 350° for about 35 minutes or until set.

••••

Creamy Beets

1 can quartered beets
2–3 T. sour cream
¼ c. zesty Italian salad dressing

Heat the beets thoroughly, drain well, and toss with the remaining ingredients.

••••

Bootstrap Potatoes

These baked potatoes are crusty and showy and dress up a meal of burgers, meatloaf, or chops. Peel and boil the potatoes when you have time, several days in advance if you like. Tuck them away in the refrigerator for this treat.

6 lg. Idaho baking potatoes
Soft butter
1 c. cornflake crumbs
12 strips bacon

Peel the potatoes and boil them whole until just barely tender. Don't overcook. Chill. Using soft butter or margarine and your bare hands, coat the potatoes. Then roll them in the cornflake crumbs. Wrap each with two slices of bacon in a cross, tucking ends in well, and bake on a cookie sheet at 375° about 20 minutes or until the bacon is just crisp.

••••

Turn cornbread mix into a zesty vegetable side dish. Sauté 2 large onions in butter until soft. Spread in baking pan and cover with cornbread batter. Bake until bread tests done, and serve with a spoon.

Vegetables as a Main Dish

Spinach-stuffed Shells

This is the ideal first-night-out dinner because you can assemble it completely at home. Whisk it out of the refrigerator and into the oven. By the time you're hooked up and settled in, it will be meltingly fragrant and ready to eat.

2 pkgs. frozen spinach (total 20 ounces)	1 T. dried parsley flakes
8 oz. shredded mozzarella	1 t. mixed Italian herbs
1 pint cottage cheese	32-oz. jar spaghetti sauce
½ c. grated Parmesan cheese	Additional grated Parmesan
3 T. dried onion flakes	12 jumbo pasta shells

Thaw spinach in a sieve to drain thoroughly. Press to remove remaining moisture. Mix with all other ingredients except sauce and shells. Boil the shells according to the manufacturer's directions until barely soft. Cool and stuff with spinach mixture. Pour half the spaghetti sauce into a 13 X 9 X 2-inch baking dish and arrange shells on top. Cover with remaining sauce and sprinkle with cheese. Cover with plastic wrap and refrigerate. Bake, uncovered, at 350° for 45–60 minutes. Serves 4–6.

●●●●

Squash Flapjacks

Serve these with ketchup for a simple supper. Add sausage patties if you want a meat, steamed carrots for color contrast, and hot apple pie for dessert.

2 c. shredded zucchini or summer squash
½ c. flour
2 eggs, slightly beaten
Salt, pepper
Cooking oil

Mix everything in a bowl and cook as you would pancakes, in a hot skillet, using about ¼ inch of hot oil. Brown on both sides, drain on paper towels, and serve at once. Serves 2–4.

●●●●

Cheese-topped Baked Potatoes

4 lbs. baking potatoes
½ stick butter
1 clove garlic, mashed
Small onion, minced
3 T. instant-blend flour

1 t. Dijon mustard
12 oz. beer
12 oz. grated cheddar
4 T. real bacon bits (optional)

Bake the potatoes, cut a cross in the centers, and squeeze to open and fluff them. To make the sauce, sauté the garlic and onion in the butter, then blend in the flour, mustard, and beer and stir over low heat until it's thickened. Gradually add the cheese, cooking just until it melts. Sauce potatoes with the cheese mixture and sprinkle each with a tablespoon of the bacon.

●●●●

Baked Potato Campfire Dinner

4 lg. baking potatoes
2 pkgs., 9 oz. each, creamed spinach
Pinch nutmeg
4 eggs
Grated Parmesan cheese (optional)

Scrub the potatoes, wrap in foil, and bake them on the grill until tender. Thaw the spinach. Carefully open the foil, leaving each potato surrounded by a "boat" of foil. Cut a cross in the top of each potato and spread it open.

Spoon the creamed spinach into the potatoes, make a nest in each bed of spinach, sprinkle very lightly with nutmeg, and break an egg into each. Put the potatoes back on the grill or in the coals, lidding lightly with foil if the day is windy, just until eggs are poached to the desired doneness. Sprinkle with cheese and eat right out of the foil. Complete this meal with raw vegetable sticks, a low-calorie yogurt dip, and big oatmeal raisin cookies for dessert. No dishes to wash!

●●●●

Ratatouille Pizza

1 can dough for 12-inch
   pizza, unbaked
¼ c. olive oil
Small eggplant, peeled
   and diced
Med. zucchini, diced
Med. onion, diced

2 cloves garlic, mashed
2 t. mixed Italian herbs
8-oz. can tomato sauce
½ t. salt
¼ c. freshly grated
   Parmesan cheese
4 oz. grated mozzarella cheese

Remove the pizza dough from the can and unroll onto a lightly greased pizza pan. In a roomy skillet, sauté the vegetables in the olive oil until they are just tender. Stir in the tomato sauce and seasonings and spread over the pizza dough. Sprinkle with cheese. Bake at 450° for 20 minutes, or until the dough has browned around the edges.

●●●●

Cut up 2–3 slices bacon and fry out. Pour off all but 3 T. fat, and stir-fry a medium head of red cabbage, coarsely grated. Season to taste with vinegar, salt, pepper, and a touch of sugar.

Baked Onions

When apple-sweet onions are available along roadsides in Georgia, Florida, and Texas, buy them in 10-pound sacks because you'll be using them cooked and raw in so many ways.

4 jumbo sweet onions
2 t. melted butter

Peel and trim the onions, cut in half, and arrange cut side up in a buttered casserole. Drizzle with butter, then spread with one of the following:

- •1 can any condensed cream soup mixed with 1 t. curry powder
- •⅓ c. brown sugar with ¼–½ t. cayenne pepper
- •1 c. sour cream with 1 t. dill weed
- •½ c. barbecue sauce plus ¼ c. more after foil is removed

Cover with foil and bake at 350° for 20–30 minutes or until onions are just tender but still hold their shape. Remove foil and bake another 5 minutes. Serves 8.

••••

Tomato and Celery Scallop

2 slices bacon, cut up
Lg. onion, diced
Bunch celery, cleaned and sliced
1-lb. can stewed tomatoes, broken up
1 T. instant-blend flour
2 T. water

In a roomy skillet, fry out the bacon, then add the onion and celery and cook until they begin to get tender. Add the tomatoes, cover, and simmer over low heat until the vegetables are soft. Mix the flour and water together to blend, then add to the vegetables. Bring to a boil and cook until the sauce has thickened.

••••

Eggplant Surprise

2 lbs. eggplant
2 med. onions
2 T. butter
8-oz. can applesauce

Peel and dice the eggplant. Dice the onions. Cook them together in a covered saucepan, with a little water, until very tender. Drain and mash with the butter, the applesauce, and salt and pepper to taste.

••••

Gussied-up Canned Carrots

When you're out of fresh carrots, delve into your cupboards for canned. Then make them sit up and sing by fixing them this way. Onions, frazzled in real butter, are another good way to refresh canned carrots, potatoes, spinach, or green beans.

2–3 ribs celery
1 T. butter
1 T. sesame seeds
1 can whole baby carrots

Sauté celery in butter over low heat until crisp-tender. Add sesame seeds and continue sautéing, then add well-drained carrots and stir-fry over low heat until well heated.

••••

Creamed Potatoes

2 lbs. potatoes, pared and diced
2 T. butter
2 c. milk
5 T. instant-blend flour
Freshly ground pepper
½ t. dill weed or 2 T. freshly grated Parmesan cheese

Cook the potatoes in salted water until just tender but still able to hold their shape. Drain and add the butter. Mix the milk and flour together, pour over the potatoes, and cook over low flame, stirring gently, until a thick sauce forms. Add pepper and dill weed or cheese.

••••

Unbeatable Beets

1 lb. red cabbage, coarsely shredded
1-lb. can julienne beets
1-lb. can pie-sliced apples
1 t. sugar
Salt to taste
2 T. butter

Cook the cabbage in a covered pot in a little water just until it's tender. Then fold in the drained beets, the apples, sugar, and salt. Cook over very low flame until everything is heated through. Top with butter.

Note: Make sure you buy canned apples, not apple pie filling, which contains sugar and thickener. Variation: Omit the sugar and add ¼ cup red currant jelly instead.

••••

The Best Baked Beans

The more varieties of beans I add, the better my guests like my "from scratch" baked beans. And the bigger the crowd, the more different cans of beans I can add. It's my campground potluck favorite, limited only by the size of whatever pot I have available for oven or camp-fire use. Mix canned pork and beans, light and dark red kidney beans, navy beans, pintos, chili beans, black beans, limas, perhaps even a can of garbanzos and some pigeon peas, all in their own juices. Save room for a can of pineapple tidbits in their juice. Then stir in black-strap molasses until the mixture is a rich, deep brown. Paste a couple of strips of bacon across the top and bake it uncovered at 350° until the bacon is done and the beans have formed a thick sauce, about 30 to 60 minutes. The longer the baking time, the better, but keep the beans from burning or getting too dry.

●●●●

Garlic Custard Cups

3 green peppers
3 cloves garlic, minced
2 c. milk
½ t. salt
3 eggs
Freshly ground pepper
Dash nutmeg

Cut the peppers in half, remove seeds, and take a tiny slice off the bottom if necessary so they will lie flat. Arrange the pepper halves in a lightly greased baking pan. Scald the milk with the minced garlic until a skin forms on top. Beat the eggs with the salt, pepper, and nutmeg. Strain the hot milk into the eggs, beating well, and pour into the pepper cups. Bake at 350° for 20–30 minutes or until the custard is just set. Serve at once with meat hot from the grill.

●●●●

Bubble and Squeak

A mainstay of British pub fare, this all-in-one vegetable dish is ideal for the space-short RV galley.

Small onion, diced
3 T. oil (traditionally, beef or bacon fat is used)
2 cans (1 lb. each) sliced potatoes, rinsed and drained
1-lb. can sliced carrots, drained
Small cabbage, shredded
Worcestershire sauce to taste

If you're using fresh potatoes and carrots, cut them up and boil until tender. Sauté the onion in hot fat in a large skillet. Add the other vegetables and stir-fry them until the cabbage is wilted and the potatoes are lightly browned. Add the Worcestershire sauce, then salt if needed.

●●●●

Fast Lane

•Roll leftover steamed vegetables in crescent rolls, bake until the rolls are brown and crusty, and serve as a main dish or side dish. Add a cheese sauce if you like.

•Steam carrot chunks until tender, and toss with a little brown sugar, a few tablespoons of raisins, and a nugget of butter to coat the carrots.

•Make vegetarian stuffed peppers by filling green pepper halves with canned Spanish rice. Sprinkle with grated cheese and bake until the peppers are crisp-tender.

•Make a zesty vegetarian pizza by spreading toasted English

muffin halves with pesto (from the grocer's refrigerated section). Broil just until heated.

• Fill a big, buttered casserole with drained canned sweet potatoes and spread with canned apple pie filling. Bake until heated through.

• Make a 2-in-1 vegetable by boiling potatoes with turnips, cabbage, or carrots. Mash with plenty of butter and season to taste.

• Make white sauce from a package and fold in quartered whole potatoes from a can and 2 c. frozen peas, thawed. Heat through.

CHAPTER FOURTEEN

Your Salad Days

The crunch of lettuce, bursting with moistness. The tang of freshly picked nasturtium leaves. Tender dandelion shoots, young mustard greens, and pokeweed salad made under the direction of a native who knows its secrets. . . .

Salads made fresh from local produce are another way to translate travel into mealtime pleasure. Dare to discover new greens and ingredients as you go. Locals love to talk about their regional specialties, enriching your roster of friends as your knowledge grows.

This section is divided into two parts. One lists main-dish salads. The other suggests salads to accompany the meal. Many of them are well suited for make/take preparation. Arrange the salad in a lidded plastic container with whatever garnishes you like, and refrigerate. At mealtime, simply pop off the lid and put the presentation on the table or serve in individual lettuce cups.

If you're going out for only two or three days, wash all salad greens well at home, drain, and seal in a plastic bag with plenty of air (as a protective cushion) and a couple of paper towels (to absorb excess moisture). They'll stay crisp for days.

159

Salads To Make the Meal

Beefsteak Salad

2 lbs. sirloin steak,
   seasoned and broiled
1 lb. fresh mushrooms
2 big, ripe tomatoes
Sweet onion, in rings

Small green pepper
Small red sweet pepper
14-oz. can hearts of palm
½ c. Italian dressing
Lettuce cups

Cool the steak, chill, and slice very thin across the grain. In a large bowl place the meat, sliced mushrooms, seeded and diced tomatoes, onion rings, pepper wedges, and hearts of palm, which you have cut into coin-size pieces. Toss with dressing and keep cold. To serve, toss again and spoon into lettuce cups.

●●●●

Paella Salad

5-oz. package yellow rice mix
½ lb. cooked, cleaned shrimp
Small can crab, picked
   over and drained
Small can white-meat chicken
Med. tomato, diced
½ c. fresh or thawed
   green peas

3–4 scallions, thinly sliced

Dressing:
¼ c. vinegar
¼ c. olive oil
½ t. curry powder
Shake until well mixed.

Cook the rice according to package directions, but without the butter. Cool. Lightly toss ingredients with the dressing and serve atop a bed of Boston lettuce. Garnish with lemon wedges. Complete a cold meal by serving slabs of a hearty whole grain bread with sweet butter and fresh fruit for dessert. In cooler weather, start the meal with a cream soup and end it with mugs of hot Jack

Daniels coffee. (Mix ½ ounce Jack Daniels with ½ ounce Amaretto, fill the cup with hot coffee, and top with whipped cream.)

●●●●

Couscous Salad

You can substitute rice, but it's more fun to experiment with couscous, a small, pasta-like wheat product used in North African cooking. It's found in specialty food stores and keeps on the shelf as well as any pasta. This exotic, tangy salad is served warm or at room temperature.

12 oz. boneless, skinless chicken breast	3–4 scallions, finely sliced
Water	1 T. peanuts, chopped
1 carrot, coarsely grated	2 T. lemon juice
1 c. couscous	1 T. olive oil
6 radishes	1 t. ground cumin
½ c. raisins	1 t. ground turmeric
	Salt, pepper to taste

Poach the chicken in about 2 cups boiling water until it's thoroughly done. Drain, saving 2 tablespoons of the liquid for the salad dressing, and set the remaining liquid aside. Cool chicken and cut into bite-size morsels. Bring 1½ cups of the poaching liquid to a boil, stir in the carrot and couscous, cover, and remove from heat. Let stand 5 minutes, then fluff with a fork. Toss together the couscous, chicken, vegetables, and nuts. Whisk together the remaining ingredients plus the reserved poaching liquid and toss with the couscous mixture. Serves 4–6.

●●●●

Add a few tablespoons of salad dressing to a plastic bag of salad greens, toss, and serve. Throw away the bag. No salad bowl to wash!

Pasta Crab Salad

This is easily made at home. Pile it into a pretty carry-serve container and keep it cold. Serve within a day or two.

1 lb. small seashell pasta,
   cooked and drained
12 oz. imitation crab
   meat, cut up
2 hardboiled eggs, diced
3 stalks celery, diced
Lg. carrot, grated

½ green bell pepper, diced
½ red sweet pepper, diced
Small sweet onion, diced
½ c. green peas, thawed
½ c. yogurt
½ c. mayonnaise

Mix pasta, crab, and vegetables in a large bowl. Whisk together mayonnaise and yogurt and toss with remaining ingredients. Add salt and pepper to taste. Garnish with lemon wedges. Complete each plate with a slice of chilled tomato aspic, slabs of French bread, and a pat of sweet butter. Add a dry white wine if you like. Fresh cantaloupe goes well for dessert.

••••

Macaroni Salad, Master Recipe

Macaroni is a mainstay, especially during the summer when you can make a mountain of macaroni salad at home and bring a batch out of the refrigerator for lunch daily during the first two or three days of your trip. Make sure the refrigerator stays at 40°–45°, and package the salad in batches so you take out only enough for each meal, keeping the rest cold.

The first day, serve it with deli cold cuts and garnish with spiced apple rings. The second, strew it with drained tuna and serve with sliced tomato aspic. The third, dice and mix in a can of ham and serve with pineapple rings.

This makes 3 batches of 4 servings each.

1-lb. box macaroni
1 c. mayonnaise
1 c. yogurt
1 t. dried dill
Sweet red onion, diced

Sweet green pepper, diced
Sweet red pepper, diced
3 T. sweet pickle relish
3 ribs celery, diced

While the macaroni is cooking, mix the other ingredients in a big bowl. Drain the macaroni when it's cooked just tender, not mushy, and fold it into the other ingredients. Divide into storage containers, and chill at once.

●●●●

Salads To Go with the Meal

Pasta Salad, Master Recipe

Cook 8 ounces of your favorite pasta, then add your choice of the following:

4 oz. fresh snow peas, trimmed
1 med. sweet or Bermuda
  onion, finely diced
2 stalks celery, diced
½–1 c. red and green
  pepper, diced
2 large carrots, grated
½ c. frozen peas, thawed

2–3 canned artichoke hearts,
  drained and quartered
2 med. tomatoes, seeded and
  diced
¼ c. sliced ripe olives or ¼ c.
  stuffed olives, sliced
⅓ c. pecans or cashews

Toss with your own variation of the master dressing, below.

●●●●

Use fruited yogurt as a quick, low-calorie dressing on fruit salad.

Master Dressing

½ c. salad oil
¼ c. vinegar
Salt, pepper to taste

Vary this basic dressing by adding fresh or dried basil, or 1 tablespoon soy sauce and a pinch of ginger, a dash of onion or garlic salt, 1 tablespoon Dijon mustard, 1 teaspoon sugar, or 1 tablespoon tomato paste. Experiment with various salad oils and different vinegars— red wine vinegar for a robust flavor, tarragon vinegar for an exotic aroma, lemon juice for a fruity tartness. Whisk ingredients together in a large bowl, add remaining salad ingredients, and toss lightly.

●●●●

Right Now Corn Relish

Corn relish is a perfect complement to almost any main dish, and it's a life-saver when fresh salads aren't available. Here's a tangy, instant version to stir up in your RV when you have a yen for corn relish and a need for a special fillip on a simple meal.

1 can whole corn with red peppers
1 stalk celery
Small red onion
¼ green pepper
1 T. brown sugar
⅓ c. vinegar
1 T. prepared mustard
Salt if needed

Drain the corn and put it in a serving dish. Finely mince the vegetables and stir them into the corn with the other ingredients. It's now ready to serve but will get better with chilling.

●●●●

Marinated Fennel Salad

Fennel tastes somewhat like celery with a faint taste of anise. This salad is something different, refreshingly crisp and cold.

2 lg. fennel bulbs
2 t. lemon juice
1 cucumber
2 scallions
Salt
8 oz. radishes
2 T. vinegar
6 T. oil

Wash, trim, and halve the fennel bulbs and slice them thinly, as for celery. Peel and seed the cucumber, slice it, and sprinkle with salt. Let stand 45 minutes, and drain it on paper toweling. Trim and slice the radishes; slice the scallions. Toss the vegetables together, then shake the vinegar, lemon juice, and oil together and pour over the salad. Toss again and refrigerate. Garnish with chopped fresh parsley if you have some. Makes 4 salad servings.

●●●●

Slow-Lane Slaw

There are many variations of this cole slaw, which keeps in the refrigerator for a week or more. This version has no oil. Its secret is a cooked dressing that does not get watery. I make a large batch of it at home, using the food proces-

sor, and vary it during the week by topping it with diced apple one day, and grated carrot topping with a sprinkling of fresh chopped parsley the next day.

Lg. head cabbage, about 3 lbs.	1 c. sugar
Med. sweet onion	1 c. vinegar
3 ribs celery	1 t. turmeric
1 bell pepper	1 t. mustard seed

Grate the vegetables fine or coarse, as you like them. Mix the sugar, vinegar, mustard seed, and turmeric in a small saucepan and bring to a boil. While the mixture is still warm, toss it with the cabbage. Refrigerate slaw for 24 hours to allow flavors to blend. Mix before serving.

●●●●

Sticks and Stones Salad

This salad too improves as it marinates. And it's made from canned vegetables, after you run out of lettuce.

1 lb. can whole green beans	Lg. sweet onion, in rings
Small jar pimientos	1 c. sugar
4 ribs celery, sliced	½ c. salad oil
into matchsticks	¾ c. vinegar
1 can baby carrots	1 t. salt
1 bell pepper	

Drain canned vegetables and toss lightly together with the onion rings, diced pepper, and celery. Bring the sugar, oil, vinegar, and salt to a boil, pour over the vegetables, cool, and refrigerate overnight.

●●●●

When you finish a big jar of pickles, bring the leftover juice to a boil and pour it over a pile of carrot sticks. Refrigerate overnight, and you'll have dilly carrots.

Vegetables Vinaigrette

Make this a day or two ahead of time at home, and serve it instead of a hot vegetable with meat from the grill. It is tangy and colorful. To make a meatier salad to serve as a vegetarian main dish, use a larger can of garbanzos.

1 head cauliflower	1 sweet red pepper
1 head broccoli	Bunch scallions
3 carrots	8-oz. can garbanzos, drained
3 ribs celery	Small can sliced ripe olives, drained
1 bell pepper	Lettuce cups for serving (optional)

Trim and cut up all the vegetables into bite-size chunks and place in a large pot.

Make a dressing from:

1 c. wine vinegar	1 T. dried parsley
1 c. water	1½ t. mixed Italian herbs
⅓ c. virgin olive oil	Freshly ground pepper
2–3 cloves garlic, finely minced	½ t. salt

Bring the vegetables to a boil in this dressing, reduce heat, cover, and simmer 5 minutes. Turn into a covered container suitable for carrying and serving, and refrigerate overnight. To serve, use a draining spoon to lift the vegetables from the dressing and arrange them in lettuce cups. Add garbanzos and olives.

●●●●

Stretch dwindling lettuce supplies by adding well-drained canned foods to tossed salads. Good additions include artichoke hearts, whole green beans, garbanzos, sliced beets, black beans, plain or marinated mushrooms, or baby carrots.

Tofu Egg Salad

This makes enough for a crowd, and nobody will guess that healthful, low-fat bean curd has been used as a partial stand-in for cholesterol-heavy eggs.

8-oz. block tofu
6–8 hardboiled eggs
6 ribs celery, finely diced
Small onion, minced
2–3 T. pickle relish (optional)
Small carrot, grated
1 c. nonfat yogurt
Mayonnaise

Mash the tofu and eggs together and fold in the celery, onion, and relish. Add the yogurt and stir well, then add mayonnaise to reach the desired moistness. Serve by the scoop as a main-dish salad or use it as a sandwich filling.

••••

Golden Glow Salad

2 c. carrot rotelle or other carrot pasta
6 hardboiled eggs
Lg. yellow sweet pepper, diced
Med. Spanish onion, minced
4 oz. shredded cheddar cheese
1 T. Dijon mustard
8-oz. carton nonfat lemon yogurt
Mayonnaise

Boil the pasta in salted water until it's just tender. Drain. Fold in the remaining ingredients, ending with the mayo, little by little, until it is moistened to your family's taste. Serve on lettuce-lined plates if you like. Serves 6–8.

••••

Sausage Salad

1 lb. head cabbage
1 lb. head red cabbage
2 med. cucumbers
2 lbs. mixed lunch meats, in chunks*
2 tomatoes, seeded and diced
1-lb. can sliced potatoes, rinsed and drained
Small, sweet onion, minced
½ c. Italian dressing

*Get a good variety of fully cooked deli meats, including smoked sausage, wursts, salami, kielbasa, boiled ham, etc.

At home, coarsely shred the cabbage, slice the cucumbers, and place in a colander. Sprinkle with salt and let drain, pressing lightly to remove excess moisture. Dice meats. Toss sausage and vegetables lightly with dressing and keep cold. Toss again just before serving. Complete the meal with buttered pumpernickel rolls, perhaps a mug of instant soup if the night is cold, and individually wrapped pie-style cookies.

••••

Use-Your-Noodle Salad

Med. green pepper, diced
1 lb. pkg. grated cabbage for slaw (or shred a 1-lb. cabbage)
3–4 scallions, finely sliced
½ lb. chunk deli ham or breast of turkey
1 can chow mein noodles
½ c. Italian dressing

Pile the vegetables into a roomy bowl. Cut the meat in matchsticks and add with half the chow mein noodles. Toss with the dressing and serve at once, sprinkled with the remaining noodles.

••••

Bread Salad

Crunchy texture contrast is this crusty salad's appeal, so serve it immediately after mixing. It goes well with cold cuts, wursts, pasta casseroles, or any hot meat.

2 c. plain croutons
3 lg. fresh tomatoes
⅓ c. Italian dressing

Toss the croutons with the diced tomatoes and the dressing, and serve at once. Serves 4–6.

●●●●

SOS: Meals from Shelf Staples

There's a snug, smug feeling in knowing that you have an extra meal or two in your RV cupboards, ready to pull out if you want to linger longer in a pleasant campsite or invite the neighbors in for an impromptu meal. Thanks to modern canned and packaged goods, you can keep a complete menu or two on hand.

Plan one complete meal, keep all the ingredients together in one locker, and don't let yourself raid these supplies for other uses. Here are complete menus that stay ready on your shelf for weeks yet come to the galley table looking fresh and coordinated. If you have fresh foods available, of course, use them to supplement the canned and packaged ones.

Sweet-and-Sour Spam Scramble

1-lb. can whole potatoes
2 T. butter
12-oz. can "light" luncheon meat
1-lb. can garbanzo beans, drained
1-lb. jar sweet-and-sour red cabbage
2 T. onion flakes
1 packet sour cream mix

171

Rinse the potatoes and cut them into quarters. Dice the lunch meat. Heat the butter to bubbling, then frazzle the potatoes and meat to brown them slightly. Add the beans, cabbage, and onion, cover, and steam over low heat until everything is well heated and the onions have softened. Top each serving with a dollop of sour cream, made according to package directions. Serves 4.

Complete the meal with hot bread from a boxed mix, apricot jam, whole asparagus spears heated in the can, and canned tapioca pudding sauced with Tia Maria for dessert.

••••

Salmon Frittata

6-serving packet instant mashed potatoes
2 T. onion flakes
½ t. dill weed
2 eggs
Oil for frying
1-lb. can salmon, drained and picked over

Add the onion flakes to the potatoes in a bowl, and add hot water, milk, and butter as directed on the potato package. Cool. Stir in the eggs and dill weed. Heat the oil in a big, nonstick skillet and spread the potato mixture evenly on the bottom. Drop the salmon by spoonfuls over the potatoes. Press in lightly but do not stir. Cover and cook over low heat until the mixture is "set" and crusty on the bottom. Slip it onto a plate, add a little more oil to the pan, then flip the frittata back into the pan to brown the other side. Cut into 4 wedges and serve.

To complete the menu add pickled beets from a jar, canned peas with small onions, rye hardtack with butter, and canned plum pudding with a jar of hard sauce for dessert.

●●●●

Black Beans and Rice

2, 1-lb. cans black beans
1 lb. canned ham
4 servings white rice
1 jar hot and spicy salsa

Empty the black beans into a saucepan, juice and all. Dice half the ham into pea-size pieces, saving the other half for another meal. Heat the beans and ham, seasoning them with a touch of the salsa, until bubbly. Cook your favorite rice in your favorite way, then mix in 1–2 tablespoons of the salsa. Fill 4 dinner plates with rice and ladle with the bean mixture. Pass the remaining salsa so each diner can add it to taste. Add side dishes of canned tomatoes topped with crunchy croutons, warmed canned tortillas as your bread, and a juicy dessert such as canned mandarin oranges drifted with coconut.

●●●●

Chickenoodle Mediterranean

If you don't usually carry these items on board, seal them in a small plastic bag at home:

2 T. dried bell pepper flakes
½ t. garlic granules
2 T. dried onion flakes
½ t. mixed Italian herbs

Keep this on your RV's emergency shelf with:

12-oz. package egg noodles
3 cans, each about 7 oz., chunk chicken
28-oz. can stewed tomatoes
1-lb. can tiny green peas
6-oz. can pitted ripe olives

Bring a large pot of water to a boil and cook egg noodles according to package directions. Drain. Stir in dried herbs and remaining ingredients except peas and olives, cover, and cook over very low heat until everything is heated through. Turn off the heat and let stand 5 minutes more. Gently fold in drained peas and pile it all into a serving bowl, then strew with sliced ripe olives. Serve any fresh raw vegetables you can manage, plus buttery crackers, pear halves sprinkled with (canned if necessary) julienne carrots, and, for dessert, canned chocolate pudding crowned with raspberry liqueur.

●●●●

Tortellini a GoGo

7-oz. pkg. tricolor tortellini with cheese filling
3 c. water
3 beef bouillon cubes
1-lb. can baby carrots, drained
1-lb. can zucchini in tomato sauce
1-lb. (more or less; brands vary) can cannellini beans
1 t. mixed Italian herbs

Cook the tortellini according to package directions until just tender. Drain it, saving the water to help make up the 3 cups needed now. Put 3 cups water in the pot with the tortellini and bring to a boil. Add bouillon, carrots, undrained zucchini and beans, and herbs. Simmer until everything is well blended and heated through. Add salt and pepper to taste. Serve in shallow soup bowls. Makes 4 servings.

Complete the meal with packaged cheese bread sticks, a robust red wine, and a salad of canned mushrooms and canned artichoke hearts marinated in a light vinaigrette. For dessert, arrange canned baked apples in serving dishes, then drizzle with butterscotch ice cream topping from a jar.

•••

Cranbake Hambake

2 T. raisins
¼ c. rum or brandy
4 servings top-of-stove stuffing mix
1-lb. canned ham
1-lb. can whole cranberry sauce

Heat the rum or brandy, add the raisins, and soak them while you proceed. Make up the stuffing mix according to package directions and pile it lightly in a buttered baking pan. Cut the ham into 4 slabs and arrange atop the stuffing mix. Mash together the cranberry sauce, raisins, and remaining rum or brandy and spread over the ham. Bake at 350° for about 25 minutes, or until everything is well heated and a light crust has begun to form where the stuffing meets the sides of the buttered pan. Cut into 4 squares and serve with chunky apple-sauce, succotash from a can, and cornbread made from a box mix and drowning in honey butter.

For dessert, throw a bag of unsalted Orville Reddenbacher popcorn into the microwave. When it's done, sprinkle it lightly with cinnamon sugar.

•••

Cooked Salad Dressing

If you're out of mayonnaise or salad dressing, here is a dressing that doesn't take the large amounts of oil needed to make real mayo. It's good for people who are on low-fat diets too.

⅓ c. dry milk
1¼ t. dry mustard
1 t. salt, dash pepper
1 T. flour
1 egg

1 c. water
2 T. vinegar
1 T. butter
6 t. sugar

Combine the dry ingredients in the top of a double boiler or in a heavy saucepan over very low flame. Beat the egg with the water and vinegar, add to the dry ingredients, and cook, stirring constantly, until it's smooth and thick. Careful! It burns easily. Remove from heat and add the butter and sugar. This makes a pint of dressing, enough for a big batch of potato salad.

••••

Spaghetti Carbonara

There's always a package of spaghetti in a cupboard somewhere, but not always the sauce or sauce makings. I like this light, slightly smoky flavor as a change from the same old tomato sauces. Be sure to cook the spaghetti al dente, not too soft. Canned bacon can be used instead of real or imitation bacon bits. Fry it out, drain, and crumble it as you do fresh bacon. Keep grated cheese on the shelf but watch expiration dates.

8-oz. pkg. spaghetti
½ c. milk
1 clove garlic
1 T. oil
⅓ c. mayo or salad dressing
1 egg
½ can or jar real bacon bits
⅓ c. freshly grated Parmesan or Romano cheese

Sizzle the minced garlic in hot oil to soften, then reduce heat and gradually stir in the milk and mayo. Heat well but don't boil. Remove from heat and stir in the beaten egg. Add this mixture, with the bacon and grated cheese, to the hot, cooked spaghetti, toss, and serve at once. Serves 4.

Complete the meal with hot bread made from a roll mix on your shelf, marinated Italian vegetables from a jar (or a green salad if you can manage one), then an SOS shelf dessert like this one:

●●●●

Honey Rice Dessert

1 c. brown or white rice
2 c. water
⅓ c. raisins
⅓ c. chopped walnuts
Dash apple pie spice
⅓ c. chopped, pitted dates
Honey or maple syrup

Cook the rice according to package directions until soft. Remove from heat and stir in everything but the honey. Cover and set aside so flavors will blend and dates and raisins will absorb moisture. To serve, spoon into bowls and drizzle with honey or syrup.

●●●●

Don't forget to include breads among emergency foods. They include hot roll or cornbread mix, packaged crackers and bread sticks, rusks, and canned tortillas or Boston brown bread. Shelf-stable spreads include peanut butter, cheese spreads (unopened), and honey.

Beer and Bacon Soup

You don't have to like beer to enjoy this remarkably hearty hot soup. Cooked, crumbled real bacon bits are one of the mainstays of my emergency shelf.

1 c. water
1 chicken bouillon cube
12-oz. can beer
16-oz. jar Cheese Whiz
2 c. water
⅔ c. dry milk
½ can or jar real bacon bits
3 T. cornstarch
Tabasco

Heat a cup of water in a saucepan and add the bouillon cube. Add the beer and continue heating the pan. Meanwhile, in a paper cup, gradually add water to the dry milk and cornstarch to make a paste. Add this to the beer mixture with the remaining 2 cups of water. Cook, stirring, until thick. Stir in cheese over low heat until mixture is smooth. Do not boil. Spoon into bowls and sprinkle generously with bacon bits. Pass Tabasco, which can be added to taste. Serves 3–4.

If you have a package of pilot crackers on the shelf, enjoy them with the soup. Then bring out a package of guava paste and some cream cheese to spread on the crackers for dessert. Pass a bowl of crisp apples, and the meal is complete.

●●●●

If you keep a can of walnuts and one of ready-to-eat pitted dates on the shelf, you can make a toothsome dessert by stuffing each date with a walnut half, then rolling it in sugar.

Salmon Mousse

Delicate, nutritious salmon in cans stays ready on your shelf until needed. A small jar of mayo, squirreled away for emergencies, is also a good insurance policy because it can be used in so many ways. If you have nonfat yogurt on hand, use a cup of it in this recipe instead. Results will be much the same, but calories will be cut.

1 envelope gelatin	1 sweet onion
½ c. boiling water	1 T. dill weed
Juice of ½ lemon	1-lb. can salmon, drained
Dash salt	8-oz. jar mayonnaise

Put the gelatin in a bowl with the lemon juice to soften, then add the boiling water and stir until the gelatin is dissolved. Mash in salmon and finely minced onion, stir in other ingredients, and place in 4-cup pan or bowl. Chill until set, then spoon into lettuce cups. Serve with lemon wedges, melba toast, and fresh pineapple fingers.

••••

Can-Can Quiche

It tastes so fresh and fragrant, you'll forget that it began with a can of this, a can of that.

1 stick oleo	10-oz. can cut asparagus
1 c. flour, plus	8-oz. can diced carrots and peas
Small can (⅔ c.) evaporated milk	6-oz. chunk ham
	Small onion, minced
4 eggs	½ c. grated cheddar cheese

Melt the oleo in a deep 9- or 10-inch pie plate and stir in flour to make a dough dry enough to press around bottom and sides of the plate. Flute the edges with floured fingers. Add water to the milk to make 1 cup and whisk with eggs until well mixed. Drain the vegetables well and sprinkle them on bottom of the lined pie plate. Flake the ham and sprinkle it in, then add onion and cheese. Pour the egg mixture over all and bake at 375° about 45 minutes, or until the quiche tests done. (The filling should be set, like custard, the edges of the crust should be golden brown, and a knife inserted near the center should come out clean. Do not overcook.) Let stand a few minutes, then cut into wedges. Serves 4–6.

●●●●

Pasta Primavera

Canned vegetables are no substitute for fresh, especially in a pasta primavera. Still, this version makes a brave showing when you're forced to make a meal from your emergency shelf. If you can add a handful of fresh broccoli or snap peas, of course, they'll make it that much better.

1 clove garlic, halved	Small onion, minced
⅓ c. virgin olive oil	12 pitted black olives, sliced
28-oz. can tomatoes,	3 T. red-wine vinegar
drained and chopped	2 t. mixed Italian seasonings
8-oz. can carrots and peas	1-lb. pkg. linguine or
8-oz. can cut green beans	other pasta, cooked
4-oz. can sliced mushrooms,	al dente
drained	

Rub the serving bowl well with the garlic, then put the garlic and all the vegetables together in a roomy pan, and toss with the vinegar and oil. Heat gently. Discard the garlic. Toss the vegetable mixture with the hot pasta and serve at once. Pass grated Parmesan or Romano cheese, add soft bread sticks, butter, and a robust red wine. Makes 6–8 servings.

●●●●

Saucy and Smart

Microwave Cheese Sauce Supreme

This velvety cheese sauce was developed by the Wisconsin Milk Marketing Board. By combining the ingredients first in a blender or food processor, you eliminate the frequent stirring that usually goes with microwaving. Make it at home in batches to warm up aboard in the microwave. It keeps up to a week in the refrigerator.

1 c. milk
2½ T. flour
2 T. butter
1 c. (4 oz.) shredded cheddar
Salt, pepper to taste

Combine ingredients in order listed, in blender or food processor. Process until smooth. Pour into a 4-cup bowl and microwave on High for 4–5 minutes, stirring once. Stir again just before serving. Serve on vegetables or meat, or combine with an 8-ounce package of macaroni, cooked according to package directions, to make a main dish for 5–6 people.

●●●●

Pineapple Salsa

This spicy and unusual sauce will make any plain, grilled meat or fish sit up and whistle Dixie. It's especially good with meaty fish such as tuna and swordfish, and with grilled chicken or pork.

2 T. oil
Small onion, diced
1 t. curry powder
2 T. minced fresh ginger root
Half a jalapeño pepper, finely minced
18-oz. can crushed pineapple, in its own juice

Sauté the onion, pepper, curry powder, and ginger in the hot oil until the onion is just tender. Stir in the pineapple and juice, and bring to a boil until everything is well blended and thoroughly hot. Serve warm or cold.

●●●●

Foolproof White Sauce

This is the base for sauces (add herbs), creamed dishes (add dried chipped beef or chopped hardboiled eggs), and many casseroles (in place of condensed cream soups).

1 c. cold milk
2 T. instant-blend flour
Dash salt
Dash pepper
2 T. butter

Stir everything but the butter together in a small saucepan, then cook, stirring, over low-medium heat until it's thick and smooth. Stir in butter.

●●●●

Pecan Fudge Sauce

Make up a couple of batches of this nutty sauce at home and seal them in boilable bags. Refrigerate up to 2 weeks. Warm up in a pan of hot water, to serve over plain cake, ice cream, or canned pudding.

¼ c. water
3 T. cornstarch
1 c. light corn syrup
¼ c. brown sugar
1 t. vanilla
1 t. imitation rum flavor
½ c. broken pecans
2 T. butter

In a small saucepan stir the water into the cornstarch, then add the syrup and brown sugar. Cook over low flame, stirring constantly, until it thickens. Stir in flavorings, butter, and pecans. Serve at once or refrigerate for future use.

●●●●

Butterscotch Sauce

This sauce transforms canned pears or a plain pound cake into a gourmet dessert.

4½-oz. pkg. instant butterscotch pudding mix
¾ c. light corn syrup
Small can evaporated milk
Water to thin

In a medium bowl combine the pudding mix, syrup, and milk and whisk thoroughly. Let stand about 10 minutes, until it thickens, then thin with water to the desired consistency.

●●●●

Gringo Green Sauce

10-oz. pkg. chopped spinach
½ c. chopped parsley
½ t. dill weed
2–3 scallions, finely diced
1 c. mayonnaise
Garlic salt to taste

Thaw the spinach and press with paper towels to remove all excess moisture; otherwise, sauce will be watery. Combine everything in a bowl (for a smoother sauce, use a food processor), adding garlic salt to taste. Serve over hot vegetables or as a dip with crackers or raw vegetables.

●●●●

Green Sauce with a Kick

Its blend of herbs is intoxicatingly delicious, and this versatile sauce gets better if flavors are allowed to chill and mingle overnight. Serve it cold over hot or cold seafood, cold cuts, boiled shrimp, or even a plain or cheese omelet. You do need a blender or food processor to make it, so if you don't have either on board, make this sauce at home to use along the way. It keeps several days in the refrigerator.

1 c. each, tightly packed, parsley sprigs, watercress leaves, and
fresh basil leaves
¼ c. pine nuts or toasted almonds
¼ c. fresh lime juice
¼ c. olive oil
2 cloves garlic
½ t. Tabasco

Process until smooth, cover, and chill 24 hours. Makes 1 cup. Stir before using.

●●●●

CHAPTER SEVENTEEN

Sweet Somethings: Desserts

Here are some sweet dreams to end your meals—indoors and out. Enjoy the fancy recipes, but don't forget those old standbys, marshmallows toasted over the campfire. Melty and warm, flavored with a whisper of wood smoke and basking in the glow of good company and a flickering fire, they are still one of life's most sumptuous desserts.

Deep South Banana Pudding

Although this has been a Southern standard for years, it may be new to you. As it chills, the wafers soften and everything blends into creamy, flavorful goo.

2 c. milk
4-serving pkg. instant vanilla pudding mix
3 ripe, firm bananas
36 vanilla wafers
1-qt. carton whipped topping

Beat milk and pudding mix together in a container that will hold at least 2 quarts. Remove 1 cup of the pudding mix, cover remaining pudding with a layer of sliced bananas, a layer of wafers, and a layer of the whipped topping. Continue layers, ending with the rest of the pudding. Seal to edges. Refrigerate several hours or overnight.

Note: Bananas are less likely to brown if slices are dipped in lemon juice or Fruit Fresh.

●●●●

Dessert Fun-do

8-ounce package cream cheese
7-oz. jar marshmallow cream
¼ c. orange juice
2 T. grated orange rind

Set out cream cheese until it's room temperature, then beat it with marshmallow cream, orange juice, and orange rind. Put the Fun-do in the center of the table, surrounded by fresh fruit—strawberries, banana chunks, pineapple chunks, apple wedges—or chunks of angel food cake. Each person spears a chunk with a fork and dips into the sauce. Tradition dictates that, if you drop your dipper in the sauce, you must kiss everyone at the table!

●●●●

Cold Oven Cookies

These quick cookie squares require no baking. They hold together better if they are cold, so make them on a chilly day or keep them in the refrigerator.

2 c. graham cracker crumbs
1 lb. confectioners sugar
16-oz. jar peanut butter
½ stick butter or oleo
16-oz. pkg. real chocolate chips

Combine the cracker crumbs, peanut butter, and sugar in a 9 X 11-inch pan and drizzle with the melted butter. (Melt it in the microwave or in a double boiler, using a container large enough to hold the chocolate chips later.) Mix thoroughly, then pat tightly into the pan in an even layer. Chill. Melt the chocolate chips and spread them over the crumb layer. Chill, then cut into squares.

●●●●

Uncookies

These easy cookies are best made with square white sandwich breads. Cut off the crusts if you want to be fancy; I don't bother. Simply cut each slice of bread into 4 strips. Pour a can of sweetened condensed milk into a shallow dish and fill another dish with sweetened, shredded coconut. Dip the bread in the milk, then coat well with the coconut and bake at 375° on a well-greased cookie sheet for 15–20 minutes or until the "cookies" are golden brown.

●●●●

Work-of-the-Devil Pie

Idle hands make sweet work in this sinfully rich and slothfully easy pie. It forms its own fudgy crust, making the cook look like a miracle worker in mere minutes. Serve it slathered with whipped cream or whipped topping. It's so dark and chocolatey, it really needs the contrast of a light, white, whipped topping.

1 stick butter
2 eggs
2 squares semi-sweet
   chocolate
½ c. flour

1 c. sugar
Splash vanilla
Dash salt
½ t. instant coffee
Whipped topping

Preheat the oven to 350° and melt the butter in a pie plate. Add the chocolate and return it to the oven just until the chocolate melts. Whisk the eggs until light, then add them with the remaining ingredients to the melted butter mixture. Mix well. Bake at 350° for 25–30 minutes and let cool at least 20 minutes before cutting.

●●●●

Nice-and-Slice Cookies

Whip these up on board or at home any time you're in the mood. The dough can wait—up to 10 days in the refrigerator, or up to 90 days in the freezer—for the day when you feel like baking. The cookies are best if made with real butter.

1 c. butter
2 c. brown sugar, firmly packed
2 eggs
1 t. vanilla
3⅓ c. flour
1 t. baking soda
1 c. finely chopped nuts, tiny chocolate chips, or coconut

Beat the butter and sugar together until light, then beat in eggs and vanilla. Combine the dry ingredients and stir them in, then stir in the nuts, chips, or coconut. On a floured towel, shape the dough into three logs. Wrap individually in plastic wrap and chill 4 hours or more. To bake, slice about ¼ inch thick and bake on ungreased cookie sheets at 375° for about 5–6 minutes. Cook thoroughly on wire racks before storing in tightly sealed containers.

●●●●

> **Don't forget:** When camping at high altitudes, all cooking times are longer.

Raspberry Chocolate Torte

1 rectangular loaf pound cake from the bakery
1 jar raspberry preserves
1 can chocolate frosting

Using a sharp bread knife, carefully cut the pound cake into 4 layers. Spread 2 with preserves, 1 with frosting, and assemble the cake. Then frost the top and sides with the remaining chocolate frosting.

●●●●

Flaming Bananas

This is one of the easiest desserts to make, yet because it is flamed, it adds a fancy finale to the meal.

10 firm bananas
2 T. lemon juice
½ c. sweetened flaked coconut
⅓ c. sugar
½ c. cognac or rum

Peel the bananas and nestle them in a buttered shallow casserole. Sprinkle with lemon juice, coconut, and sugar. Bake at 350° until the bananas are brown but not mushy. Heat the cognac or rum in a shallow skillet, pour over the bananas, and light with a match.

Make a skillet upside-down cake. Arrange pineapple slices in melted butter in a heavy 8-inch skillet. Sprinkle with brown sugar, then drizzle with a bottle of shake-and-pour pancake mix, mixed according to directions on the label. Cover, and cook over low flame until the batter is springy and set.

Coffee Custard

2 c. milk
1 c. strong, hot coffee
¾ c. light corn syrup
1 T. cornstarch
2 eggs

In a paper cup add just enough milk to the cornstarch to make a thin paste. Heat the remaining milk and corn syrup to boiling. Beat the eggs and stir them, with the hot coffee and the cornstarch mixture, into the hot milk. Cook over low flame, stirring constantly, until it thickens. Pour into 4–5 dishes and chill.

••••

Gingerbread a GoGo

Because this recipe calls for corn syrup and oil, you don't have to cream shortening and sugar. It's easy to mix by hand.

1 c. brown sugar	1 t. baking soda
3 c. flour	1 c. milk, soured with 1 t.
1 c. light or dark corn syrup	vinegar or lemon juice
1 T. ground ginger	Applesauce, canned vanilla
½ c. salad oil	pudding, or whipped cream
1 t. ground cloves	for topping

In a roomy saucepan, heat the sugar and corn syrup and stir in the oil. Shake the dry ingredients together in a bag and mix them into the oil mixture, then add the sour milk. Turn into a buttered 9 X 13-inch pan and bake at 350° for 25–30 minutes or until springy to the touch. Serve warm with applesauce, whipped cream, or vanilla pudding, or spread with vanilla frosting from a can.

••••

Eggless Cake

This is a "hard times" recipe that has been around since my grandmother's day. Its advantage for the RV cook is that it can be made without eggs and without a beater.

1 c. water	½ t. baking powder
⅓ c. shortening	1 t. soda
½ c. chopped, pitted dates	1 T. water
2 t. apple pie spice	2 c. flour
1 c. brown sugar	1 can vanilla frosting
2 c. raisins	

In a roomy saucepan, bring the water, shortening, sugar, spice, dates, and raisins to a boil for 3 minutes. Cool. Dissolve the soda in the water. Stir the soda, flour, and baking powder into the raisin mix, turn into an 8-inch pan, and bake at 350° for about 30 minutes or until springy to the touch. Cool, then frost.

●●●●

Trifling Trifle

2 individually packaged, lunchbox-size jelly rolls
2 T. sherry (optional)
2 c. milk
1 pkg. instant vanilla pudding mix

Cut each jelly roll into 4 slices and divide them among 4 dessert dishes. Better still, press them along the sides of a clear glass or plastic drinking glass, so they'll show through. Drizzle with sherry. Shake the milk and pudding mix together in a clean jar and pour into the dishes. Chill until serving time.

●●●●

Cold-Oven Peanut Butter Squares

Various recipes for boiled cookies have been around for years. In this version, the boiled batter is put into a pan and cut into squares, like fudge.

1 c. sugar
1 stick butter
½ c. water
2 t. vanilla
2½ c. raw oatmeal
2 T. powdered milk
½ c. peanut butter

Mix the sugar, butter, and water in a saucepan and bring to a full boil, then boil for 30 seconds. Remove from heat and mix in the remaining ingredients. Working quickly, spread the mixture into a buttered 8 X 8-inch pan and cool. Cut into squares.

●●●●

Cookie Crumb Cake

This is another cake that is easy to store and carry, because it is not frosted. Bake it in a 9 X 13-inch pan and cover with foil or plastic wrap. It's a good way to use up those odds and ends of cookies that get stale so quickly in the outdoor life. Just put them in a heavy-duty plastic bag, then crush them with a rolling pin.

1 yellow cake mix, prepared
    according to package
    directions
2 c. crumbs made from
    leftover cookies (or graham
    crackers)
¾ c. brown sugar
½ c. chopped walnuts
1 t. cinnamon
1½ sticks butter, melted
1 c. powdered sugar
1–2 T. water
½ t. vanilla

Make up the cake mix and pour half the batter into a greased pan. Mix the crumbs, sugar, nuts, and cinnamon. Sprinkle the batter with half the crumb mixture, carefully add the remaining batter, and top with the remaining crumb mixture. Bake at 350° for about 45 minutes or until it tests done. Cool, then make a glaze from the powdered sugar, vanilla, and enough water to make a thin frosting. Drizzle randomly over the cake and let it dry before covering.

●●●●

Bananas in a Cloud

6 ripe bananas
1 T. lemon juice
1 c. light corn syrup
1 c. sugar
2 t. apple pie spice
⅓ c. water
1 aerosol can real whipped cream

Cut the bananas in half lengthwise, then into chunks, and toss lightly with the lemon juice. Bring the corn syrup, sugar, spice, and water to a boil. Remove from heat, cool, and gently fold in the bananas. Set out 6 individual serving bowls and make a nest of whipped cream in each. Divide the banana mixture among them.

●●●●

For fitness' sake, get your family into the "walking dessert" habit. Pass out shiny apples, licorice whips, all-day suckers, Pocket Pretzels, Tootsie Pops, popcorn balls, granola bars, or other individual treats. Or stride to the campground store and buy a round of popsicles or lollipops for all.

Drizzletops

This is devious, because it's an easy way to put a homemade frill on a store-bought dessert and pass it off as your own. To make it work, you need either a small roasting bag or one of the boilable bags sold for use with meal-seal appliances.

3 oz. semi-sweet chocolate
1 T. butter

Place the chocolate and butter in the boilable bag and lower it into simmering water until it's melted. Using an oven mitt, squeeze the bag gently to mix well, dipping it in the water as necessary. Arrange the cookies, cake, or other dessert on waxed paper to catch the drips, close together so you can sweep across the lineup with an unbroken motion. Now, working quickly, snip a tiny corner from the bottom of the bag so it will leak a small stream of melted chocolate, which you now zigzag across the dessert. When you have squeezed out the last of the chocolate, throw the bag away.

••••

Zero-Calorie Desserts

Well, okay, they're not 100 percent noncaloric, but they do pack all the kick of sweet desserts with only the barest few calories. If you're diabetic, check with your dietician for exchange values. Many desserts, such as sugar-free gelatins and soft drinks, are "free" exchanges. In any case, be aware that sugar substitutes are controversial and are not for everyone.

In making diet desserts I've discovered a few tricks. For one, I find that sugarless gelatins and puddings still will set if they are made with a scant 2¼ cups water or milk instead of the 2 cups called for on the package. So you get more servings per package.

In making most desserts, I use the small, covered, plastic Rubbermaid containers that hold ½ cup each. Lids fit tightly so I don't have to worry about spills in the refrigerator, and portions are pre-measured for the dieter. This is especially helpful if you have only one person in the family who needs special desserts.

In the diet foods section of the supermarket you'll find whipped topping that is creamy, delicious, and almost "free." With one crushed dietetic cookie you can add a crumb topping to an otherwise plain diet dessert; or crush dietetic hard candies to create a tangy "sugar sprinkle" for an added burst of flavor.

I keep a bag of whole, unsugared cherries, raspberries, or strawberries in my freezer. Then I add only one or two to each serving of a sugarless gelatin or pudding. They contribute color and tang, for the "price" of only one small fruit. Or, top each serving of diet pudding with one pecan or almond half for texture contrast. The "cost" to the dieter is peanuts.

If you're on a strict diet, be sure to read labels. Some so-called dietetic or diabetic foods are sugar-free but are high in saturated fats, fructose, and other nutrients that must be "charged" to your "account."

Apricot Cream Surprise

1 package sugar-free instant vanilla pudding
¼ t. cinnamon
2¼ c. skim milk
1 jar babyfood strained apricots

Whisk pudding, cinnamon, and milk together and divide into 5 dishes or containers. Place a dollop of apricots on the center of each. Variations: babyfood apple-blueberry dessert, applesauce, or strained pears.

●●●●

Place a layer of sliced bananas in a buttered pie plate and sprinkle with lemon juice, sugar, and a little cinnamon. Drizzle with squeeze margarine and top with a solid layer of marshmallows. Bake at 350° until marshmallows are browned and puffy.

Seafoam

1 can evaporated skim milk
1 package sugarless lime gelatin
½ c. boiling water

Place the milk in a freezer tray and freeze just until ice crystals begin to form. Dissolve gelatin in water and chill until it's the consistency of egg white. Whip the milk and gelatin together with an electric beater on high speed until foamy and stiff and pour into 6 containers. Chill until firm.

•••

Ginger Peachy

1 packet unflavored gelatin
½ c. water
2 c. sugarless ginger ale
8-oz. can peaches, sugarless pack, drained
(juice may be added to the water measurement)

Soften the gelatin in the water, then heat gently until the gel dissolves. Add the ginger ale. Set out 6 containers and divide cut-up peaches among them. Add the ginger mixture and chill until set.

•••

No-Fault Ambrosia

1 pkg. sugar-free lime gelatin
8-oz. can crushed pineapple in own juice
6-oz. container 1%-fat cottage cheese

Drain the pineapple, saving the juice for another purpose. Sprinkle the dry gelatin over the cottage cheese and pineapple, and mix well. Divide into 6–8 serving containers.

●●●●

Fast Lane

•Make a quick pie crust by combining 1¾ c. uncooked oats, ½ c. flour, ⅓ c. brown sugar, and ⅓ c. melted butter. Press into a pie pan, reserving ⅓ c. of the mixture for a topping, and bake 15 minutes at 350°. Cool and fill with instant pudding, canned apple pie filling, or your favorite refrigerator cheesecake recipe. Sprinkle with reserved oat mixture and chill.

•Empty a can of applesauce into a pie plate or shallow casserole, sprinkle with sugar and cinnamon and top with a meringue made by beating 2 egg whites with ¼ c. sugar. Bake at 375° about 15 minutes or until meringue is set and browned.

•Make a canned fruit dessert more festive and lower in calories by pouring off the heavy syrup and saucing the fruit with a fizzy diet soda.

•Make a tangy topping for gingerbread or spice cake by whisking together 1 c. plain yogurt, juice of 1 small lemon, and 1 can sweetened condensed milk. Mix and spread quickly. Mixture will set like custard.

•Fill an unbaked pie shell with your choice of ready-to-bake cookie dough and bake at 350° until the crust is browned and the dough done through. Serve in wedges.

•Add a banana to your favorite bread pudding recipe before baking. Serve warm with milk or cream.

•Consider serving a dessert coffee or tea. Simply add a couple of tablespoons of liqueur to each cup. Almond or raspberry liqueur goes well with tea; brandies and cognacs with coffee.

Gifts That Say "Good-bye and Godspeed"

One of the joys of camping is that you meet a variety of people. Campground neighbors form quick friendships, but then the gladness turns to good-byes as we go our separate ways. In some cases, we may correspond with families later, or we may even conspire to meet again along the way. In rare instances, we meet again by chance. Usually, however, only the warm memories are left.

One way to keep the thread of friendship alive a little longer is to send along a food gift with the traveler. Food gifts are inexpensive and personal, and they can be given without fanfare or a feeling of obligation. Here are some food gifts that are practical to give and to receive.

Caravan Cocoa Mix

Simply bag this in any amounts you want to give away, in zip-top plastic bags trimmed with bright stickers and a label of instructions: "Put 2 tablespoons of this mixture into a cup, then fill it with boiling water and stir."

2 c. sugar
16-oz. jar coffee creamer
2 c. dry milk

1 c. unsweetened cocoa
½ c. instant coffee
1 t. cinnamon

Shake everything together in a big plastic bag until it's well mixed. Divide into smaller bags and seal well.

••••

Galliano Cocoa Mix

Unlike the powdered drink mix above, this one is a buttery paste that should be stored in the refrigerator. It will keep for up to four weeks, so make a single or double batch at home and carry it aboard to bring out in camp. To share it, portion it into pretty paper cups, wrap in plastic, and provide these instructions: "Put 1 tablespoon of this mix in a mug, fill with very hot milk, coffee, or tea, and stir. Refrigerate unused mix and use promptly."

1 c. butter (2 sticks)	½ t. almond flavor
4 c. brown sugar, firmly packed	½ t. vanilla flavor
	½ c. powdered creamer
⅔ c. Galliano liqueur	2 t. pumpkin pie spice

Real butter is best for this. Let it come to room temperature and beat in the sugar, then the other ingredients until everything is smooth and well blended. Pack into a clean, lidded container and keep it cold.

••••

Ladybugs

These are fun to make, and the children can help, but you'll have to plan ahead to have all the supplies on board. Buy the spices in bulk at a specialty shop when you see them on sale; they are much more expensive in small, supermarket packages.

Give these instructions with each bug (you'll end up with a dozen): "To make mulled cider, drop this ladybug into 6 cups of apple juice, simmer 30 minutes, then strain into mugs. (Discard the bug—whole spices could be harmful if swallowed.) Sip and enjoy!"

6 oranges, cut in half
About 2 c. brown sugar
12 cinnamon sticks
12 whole nutmegs
24 whole allspice
96 whole cloves

Dig out the orange sections, and use them for something else. Bake the orange halves on a rack, cut side up, at 250° for about 2 hours, until they are leathery. After they've cooled, pack each tightly with brown sugar.

Now picture this: Press the spices into the sugar to make a bug, with a cinnamon stick for a body, two allspice eyes, a nutmeg head, and eight clove legs. Wrap each bug tightly in plastic wrap, and store in the refrigerator. They'll keep indefinitely if the oranges were dried out enough.

●●●●

Truffles

These are best made when the weather isn't too hot and steamy, so tuck away the ingredients and bring them out on a day when you need a family project. Arranged on a pretty paper plate, they make a beautiful calling card when you are meeting new campground neighbors.

18 oz. real chocolate chips (3 bags, 6 oz. each)
14-oz. can sweetened condensed milk
1 T. vanilla
Finely chopped nuts, grated coconut,
chocolate jimmies, etc.

Melt the chocolate in the milk in the microwave (about 3 minutes) or in a double boiler. Stir in the vanilla and chill until firm and fudgy, about an hour. Shape into walnut-size balls and roll in nuts, coconut, or sprinkles.

●●●●

My Own Mustard

Conjure up a big batch of this zesty spread and divide it into clean jars. This recipe makes about 4 cups. When you give it away, recommend that it be refrigerated at once and used within a month.

⅔ c. dry mustard   1 t. dried thyme
½ c. sugar   1 t. dried basil
8 eggs   1 t. dried oregano
1 c. vinegar   1 t. dried dill weed
½ c. white wine

In a saucepan large enough to hold double the volume of this mixture, stir the mustard and sugar, then stir in the eggs, vinegar, and wine. Cook over low heat, beating continuously with a portable electric mixer until it foams up and becomes thick. It will double in size, then return to its original volume. Stir in the herbs, cool, stir, and pour into clean jars. Cover and refrigerate.

●●●●

Chutney Cheese Crock

This is a delicious way to use up bits of leftover cheese. It makes a pretty gift when packed into paper cups and topped with a layer of chopped almonds. This recipe makes 4 cups. It should be stored in the refrigerator but served at room temperature, with crackers.

2 pkgs., 8 oz. each, cream cheese   ½ c. chopped, roasted almonds
2 T. butter   (plus more for topping)
2 c. grated yellow cheese (ched-   3 T. dry sherry
    dar or whatever you have)   1 t. curry powder
½ c. chutney

Let the cream cheese and butter come to room tempera-ture in a large mixing bowl, then beat them with the other ingredients until everything is well mixed. Pack into containers and top with a layer of chopped nuts.

••••

Spiced Almonds

Almonds are economical when bought in bulk, yet they are one of nature's most elegant foods. Make up a huge batch of these toothsome nuts and package some in zip-top plastic bags for sharing.

2 c. sugar
2 t. cinnamon
Dash ground nutmeg
1 c. water
1 T. butter
2 t. vanilla
4 c. raw or roasted almonds

Boil together the sugar, spices, and water until the mixture reaches the soft ball stage, or 236° on a candy thermometer, stirring from time to time. Remove from burner, stir in butter and vanilla, then stir in the nuts. Working quickly, turn out the mixture onto waxed paper, spreading and separating to form as thin a layer as possible. Let it cool completely, then break it up into small chunks of one and two nuts each and seal in bags in giftable batches.

••••

Bloody Shame

This zippy vegetable-juice cocktail can be used as a base for Bloody Marys or enjoyed in its non-alcoholic state. It's best made a day ahead to allow flavors to blend. The secret to its tang is freshly squeezed juice. This makes about 3 quarts, to give away by the quart or pint with instructions to serve it over ice with a celery stalk swizzle, with or without a shot of vodka.

2 cans, 46 oz. each, tomato or V-8 juice
1 c. lemon or lime juice
2 T. Worcestershire sauce
Salt, pepper, hot sauce to taste
1 t. celery salt

Combine all ingredients and portion into bottles. Cover and chill thoroughly.

••••

Canny Nutbread

Rinse and dry tin cans (most aluminum cans have pull-top lids and cannot be opened with a can opener to make a clean edge) and recycle them as disposable baking pans. This makes 4 can-size loaves, one for you and three to share. Wrap and chill this bread for easier slicing, and serve in slivers for tea time or a bedtime snack.

1 stick oleo
1 c. honey
2 eggs
2 c. flour
2 t. baking powder

⅓ c. milk
A total of 1½ c. raisins, chopped
    dates, and chopped nuts in
    any combination

Cream the oleo with the honey and beat in the eggs. Add the flour and baking powder to the creamed mixture alternately with the milk, beating well. Fold in fruit and nuts. Spoon into lightly greased tins, filling each no more than ⅔ full, and bake at 350° for 30–35 minutes or until loaves test done with a toothpick. For easiest removal, let the loaves cool in the tins, then remove bottoms with a can opener and push out the bread.

••••

Popcakes

6 c. popped corn
1 c. peanuts
½ c. each raisins, sugar, light
corn syrup, peanut butter
½ t. vanilla

Do not salt or butter the popcorn. Toss it with the peanuts and raisins in a big bowl. Bring the sugar and corn syrup to a foamy boil, then remove from heat and stir in the peanut butter and vanilla. Mix with the popcorn. Press the mixture into a buttered 9 X 13-inch pan and cool until firm. Cut into squares and place each in a cupcake paper for serving or giving.

●●●●

Cheerio!

What a cheery way to say "Cheerio" to your new friends. Send them off with a box of these goodies to munch along the highway.

28 soft caramel candies
1 T. water
4 c. round oat cereal

Combine caramels and water in a small, heavy saucepan and cook over very low heat until the mixture is melted and smooth. Put the cereal in a bowl and pour in the melted caramel, tossing quickly until everything is evenly coated. Rinse hands in cold water and shape the candies into 1-inch balls. Arrange on waxed paper until set, then transfer to paper plates for giving.

●●●●

Poor Man's Pâté

This is most easily prepared in a food processor but can also be mashed together by hand. Liverwurst and cream cheese should be at room temperature for easiest mixing. It makes about 6 cups, which will fill 6–8 clear plastic cups for gift giving.

1 envelope unflavored gelatin	Small onion, finely minced
2 c. boiling water, in separate cups	1 T. chopped parsley
	Few twists freshly ground pepper
2 t. beef bouillon granules	1 c. cold water
1 lb. liverwurst	⅓ c. sherry or cognac
8-oz. pkg. cream cheese	

Sprinkle the gelatin into a cup of the boiling water and the bouillon granules into the other cup. Stir both to dissolve. Mix together the liverwurst, cream cheese, onion, parsley, and pepper, making as smooth a mixture as possible with the tools available. Stir in the gelatin, bouillon, water, and sherry and pour into individual jars or cups for giving or serving. Chill. It's served as a spread with crackers or party rye.

●●●●

Pick-Up-Your-Marbles-and-Go Fudge

1 c. light corn syrup
Small can (⅔ c.) evaporated milk
16-oz. pkg. semi-sweet chocolate
1 T. vanilla
1½ c. sifted powdered sugar
⅔ c. creamy peanut butter

Set out a 9 X 13-inch pan and line it with plastic wrap, using two or more sheets if necessary to cover bottom and sides completely. In a roomy, heavy saucepan, stir together the corn syrup and milk over very low heat, adding chocolate and stirring constantly until the chocolate is melted. Remove from heat and stir in the vanilla and sugar, then beat it with a spoon until it's smooth. Spread it into the lined pan. Working quickly while the mixture is hot, drop teaspoonfuls of the peanut butter randomly on the fudge and swirl through it with a knife to create a marbled pattern. Chill until firm, then turn out of the pan, peel off the plastic, and cut into small squares.

●●●●

Miscellaneous Tips

Baking soda is a food-quality abrasive. Use it as a cleanser, neutralizer, sweetener, and deodorizer. To clean burned-on residue from a skillet or pan, fill it with an inch of water and a tablespoon or two of baking soda. Bring it to a boil for several minutes and let it cool. The soil should lift off easily.

Bottle brush. To scrub areas you can't reach otherwise, add a few drops of detergent, warm water, and some pebbles or raw rice. Shake to scrub.

Butter corn evenly and quickly by dipping each ear in a pan of hot water in which you've melted a stick of butter. The butter floats to the top, coating the corn as you remove it.

Campfire soot cleans easily off the bottom of cookpots if you coat them first with soft bar soap.

Dishwasher detergent and a soak in very hot water are the best way to keep plastic containers sweet and odor-free. Keep your hands out of this harsh mixture.

Fat substitute. The Dannon people suggest using plain, nonfat yogurt in place of oil and eggs in brownie mix; the Mott folks suggest using applesauce instead of oil in cake mixes.

Folding dish drainers are found in camping and specialty cata-
logues. Save time and work by letting dishes air dry.

Food safety. It's easy to remember that "life begins at 40." In terms
of refrigerator safety, this means that at temperatures above 40°F,
organisms begin to grow more rapidly. Use a refrigerator thermometer
to be sure yours stays in safe ranges.

Hard-to-find foods such as organically grown canned soups,
unusual flours, and bulk items can be ordered by mail from Walnut
Acres, Penns Creek, Pennsylvania, 17862. Request a free catalogue.

Ice cream. I buy ice cream only by the pint, and it's almost never
available in this size except in space-hogging round containers. Let it
soften just enough to remove it from round tubs and press it into rectangular refrigerator containers, then place in the freezer.

Lemon juice. Bottled juice doesn't have the same punch as freshly
squeezed juice. When lemons or limes are on sale, use your electric
juicer at home to make a quart or two of juice, and freeze it in ice-cube
trays. Bag the cubes and keep them in your RV freezer.

Meatballs and hamburgers look better and cook more evenly when
they are all the same size. Here is an easy way to divide ground meat.
After completing your favorite meat mix with onions, bread crumbs,
or whatever, pile it onto a sheet of waxed paper and pat it into a flat,
even circle. Using a long knife such as a bread knife, press through the
circle to cut it in half, then in quarters. If more servings are desired, as
for meatballs, keep pressing the knife all the way across the circle to
continue dividing it into 16ths, 32nds, and so on.

Oven spills. Cut paper drinking straws in pieces and insert them as
"chimneys" in the top crust of a fruit pie. They'll prevent boil-overs.
When spills occur, sprinkle them heavily with salt. They'll dry hard
and crispy and will be easier to remove.

Paper cups are expensive and bulky to use routinely but keep some
on hand for small mixing jobs; e.g., whisking together ketchup and
grated horseradish to make cocktail sauce. Use paper plates for dredg-
ing fish in flour, mashing tofu, and other messy jobs.

Parsley. So many recipes call for a tablespoon or two of chopped,
fresh parsley. Few of us have the time and space to keep fresh herbs
aboard, yet there is no real substitute for them. I buy fresh parsley by

the bunch and chop large quantities of it at a time in the food processor or by hand. Then I pack it very lightly in small zip-top plastic bags and freeze, shaking it from time to time so it doesn't form a solid block. One bag takes up little space in the RV refrigerator, and I can scoop out a tablespoon of the flaky, frozen parsley as needed.

Poison warning. Don't use an unknown wood for green-stick cooking, planking fish, or to stir a pot over the campfire. Among poisonous woods are manchineel, found in the tropics, and such shrubs as lantana and elderberry (the wood, not the berries).

Rice. Cooked rice is ideal for many dishes that require a starch base. If you make boil-in-the-bag rice, plan to cook other boilable bags at the same time, such as vegetables in butter sauce, creamed spinach, or any homemade concoction such as beef stroganoff or creamed chicken.

Rolling pin. Slip a clean sock over a straight-sided glass bottle, and rub it with flour. For a pastry cloth, use a floured linen towel or, for small jobs such as briefly kneading biscuits, a floured paper towel. To wash, soak in *cold* water.

Rubber sink mats have many other uses in the galley. Use one in the floor of the refrigerator to dampen sound, catch spills, and prevent skidding. Don't cover refrigerator shelves with a solid material, however, or it will interfere with air circulation.

Self-rising flour. To make your own self-rising flour, add 1½ teaspoons baking powder and ½ teaspoon salt to 1 cup less 2 teaspoons flour.

Serve over. When a recipe is to be served over a starch base (e.g. creamed chicken over biscuits) and you don't want to cook another item, serve it over rice cakes, toast, or frozen waffles warmed in the toaster. Or, if you can take the salt and calories, ladle it over a bed of Chinese noodles, canned French fried onion rings, or potato sticks.

Tin-can power. Rinse cans after using, let drain, and save them to use as catch-alls, biscuit or cookie cutters, bread baking tins, and disposable pans for small tasks such as melting butter or heating syrup.

Tomato paste. If you often need just a teaspoon or two of tomato paste for recipes, open a can of it and place it by dollops on a sheet of waxed paper on a cookie sheet. Then freeze it. Put the frozen plops into a plastic bag and keep frozen to use as needed.

Tongs. Use a couple of spring-type wooden clothes pins as handles to lift a hot grill or oven rack.

Index

acorn squash and apples, 143
almonds, spiced, 203
ambrosia, no-fault, 196-97
appetizers, 65-78
    (*See also* sandwiches; snacks)
    bacon wraps, 76
    chicken McSpeedSnack, 69-70
    chutney cheese crock, 202-03
    creamy clam spread, 75
    mystery, 144
    onion pie, 69
    poor folks' pâté, 76
    poor man's pâté, 206
    shortcut soft pretzels, 77
    spiced almonds, 203
apple(s)
    acorn squash and, 143
    -topped pancakes, 28
    upset applecart, 37
applesauce
    muffins, 31
    as substitute for fat, 208
apricot
    cream surprise, 195
    scones, 49
asparagus, stir-fry, 144-45

bacon
    and beer soup, 178
    bits, 27, 49
    Canadian, in eggs Benedict, 31
    wraps, 76
baguette, sausage-stuffed, 73-74
banana(s)
    in a cloud, 193
    flaming, 189
    marshmallow, 195
    pudding, deep south, 185-86
batter, for fried fish, 100
beans
    best baked, the, 156
    rice and black, 173
    rice and calypso, 128
    Thuringer and, soup, 63
    -tomato soup, cold, 60
    tuna and, sandwiches, 71
beef
    (*See also* casseroles; meat; off-the-
        shelf meals; one-dish meals; slow
        cooking)
    corned, hashburgers, 29-30
    corned, in beer, 134

    creamed chipped, on toast, 28
    panfastic, stroganoff, 92-93
    steak Port Antonio, 89
    steak salad, 160
    Wellington, pit stop, 82
beer
    bacon and, soup, 178
    bread, more about, 52-53
    corned beef in, 134
beets
    creamy, 149
    unbeatable, 155
beverages, 19-22
    bloody shame, 203-04
    caravan cocoa mix, 199-200
    Galliano cocoa mix, 200
    liqueurs, 22
    mulled cider (ladybugs), 200-01
    nog for the 90s, 20
    posset, 21
    root beer float, 19
    slush, 21
    Turkish buttermilk, 22
    your own chocolate malt mix, 22
biscuits
    mix, 48, 63-64
    south in yo' mouth, 46-47
bran
    miller's, 37
    spoonbread with, 25-26
bran muffins
    best, the, 43-44
    Jarlsberg, 52
bread pudding
    breakfast, 23
breads, 41-54
    (*See also* muffins)
    as you like it loaf, 41
    beer, more about, 52-53
    biscuit mix, 48
    biscuits, south in yo' mouth, 46-47
    canned, 42
    carrot loaf, spicy, 45
    cornbread, vegetable, 149
    corny, 47-48
    cutting, 43
    Danish, easy cheesy, 42
    gingerbread, 51-52
    health, microwave, 43
    mixing, 50
    nutbread, canny, 204
    rolls, butterscotch pecan, 44-45